OCT 7 2003

In My Grandmother's House

Compiled & Illustrated by

BONNIE CHRISTENSEN

In My Grandmother's House

Award-Winning Authors
Tell Stories About
Their Grandmothers

HarperCollins*Publishers*

S

With very special thanks to Robert Resnik

The drypoint illustrations were inspired by exceptional photos received from our contributors and give us a glimpse into each writer's personal family album.

www.harperchildrens.com

Library of Congress Cataloging-in-Publication Data
  In my grandmother's house : award-winning authors tell stories about their grandmothers / edited and illustrated by Bonnie Christensen.
    v. cm.
  Contents: The naked truth / by Cynthia Leitich Smith — Rhizomes / by Minfong Ho — The grannies / by Pat Cummings — The doctor's daughter / by Diane Stanley — Grandma and her needle / by Beverly Cleary — A visit to Grandma's / by Gail Carson Levine — And then another locust came and took away another grain of corn / by Jean Craighead George — Granny was a gambler / by Beverley Naidoo — Fairy grandmother / by Bonnie Christensen — To my Nai Nai / by Ji-li Jiang — The best parts / by Joan Abelove — My Abuelita, my paradise / by Alma Flor Ada.
  ISBN 0-06-029109-5 — ISBN 0-06-029110-9 (lib. bdg.)
  1. Grandmothers—Juvenile literature. [1. Grandmothers.] I. Christensen, Bonnie.
HQ759.9 .I554 2003
306.874'5—dc21
                                          2002151601

Typography by Andrea Vandergrift
1 2 3 4 5 6 7 8 9 10
❖
First Edition

For Mimi, a terrific grandmother and wonderful friend
—B.C.

CONTENTS

What makes us who we are? Education? Environment? Or is it family, the sticky web of who went before, past generations, our family trees? Young faces stare out from tintype photos. Who is she? Why doesn't anyone say a word about him? Family secrets. Skeletons rattling. All of it funnels down to each of us. Some material we accept and cherish. Some we reject or deny. But even what we choose to accept or deny is influenced by our families and family history.

My grandmother once owned a large vanity with two hinged side mirrors, which I often closed around myself to create a hall of endless reflections, echoing smaller and smaller in the distance. Though initially it seemed all the images emanated from the largest, closest reflection, the longer I stood there the more it seemed equally possible that it all began with the farthest, almost infinitely small figure. Or perhaps there was no definite beginning or end at all. All I knew for sure was that my focus fell on neither the largest reflection nor the smallest, but on a reflection just a few steps away from myself; in the same space occupied by my grandmother in the chain of our family. Close enough to be comfortable but enough removed to evoke mystery.

Perhaps the mystery of grandmothers is related to the past we never knew, including the inconceivable fact that our parents were once children—our grandmothers' children. And, because grandmothers often don't live nearby, they're removed by the mysteries of both time and space. So how do they manage to seem comfortably close? Like the reflection in the mirror—not too near and not too far.

Maybe it's because grandmothers aren't responsible for us in the "Did you brush your teeth?" and "Eat your brussels sprouts!" sense. Instead, they're free to concentrate on joy and laughter, to open magical doors and light flames of curiosity, while giving us a glimpse of the past and its traditions. Grandmothers are fascinating in a multitude of respects. They own exotic objects and have different daily rituals. The food they put on the table is often as strange as the books that line their shelves, their teacups, their plants, their bathtubs, and their teeth—removable and mesmerizing, waiting in a glass of water by the bed. The question haunted me: How could she be so much "me" but also be so different, so separate?

Fascination with our grandmothers flourishes all through life, but in childhood we brag, "My dad's stronger than your dad" or "My mom's nicer than yours." So, as an adult, I was strangely surprised when a "My grandmother was more extraordinary than your grandmother" storytelling competition erupted at a writers' conference. Everyone had a story—or two—to tell. And, though we were all enchanted by each story as it was told, there was a sense that we could hardly endure the wait for our own storytelling turn. I went to sleep that night mentally laughing and wishing there was some way to gather all the stories into a collection. But how? I shelved the idea. Finally, during a meeting with Alix Reid, editorial director at HarperCollins, I summoned the nerve to offer up my half-baked grandmother anthology idea. Her enthusiasm was immediate, and she has graciously guided this anthology into existence.

The voices you will hear in these original stories are as unique and individual as the extraordinary women portrayed. The ties that bind the writers to their grandmothers range from the mystery of the identity of the "naked lady" in Cynthia Smith's story to the sense of required duty in Gail Levine's. Some of the relationships are difficult; each of them raises questions. And all will take you on journeys to times and places and into families as mysterious and comfortable as the grandmothers themselves.

It is a joy to share these stories with you and to urge you to listen to and record your own family stories. Ask your parents or grandparents for memories and family history. Dust off the tattered ancestral album. Turn the pages slowly and look into the eyes of past generations. Those eyes, those faces reflect the past centuries of struggle and hope involved in our own evolutions. Our grandmothers, and their stories, reflect not only where and whom we've come from, but where we might be going and who we might become.

CYNTHIA LEITICH SMITH

The Naked Truth

It's funny, the way you can see things pretty much your whole life but not really see them. Not just things.

People, too.

Back when we were little, my cousin Stacy Liz and I used to play in our grandparents' scrubbed cement-floor basement. We'd play camping and school and the game Operation. We'd ride on toy motorcycles 'round and 'round the furnace.

After we grew too old to play, or at least to call it that, we'd still go downstairs. On Saturdays, we'd help Grandma Dottie haul down the laundry and toss it on a line to dry. On holidays, we'd sneak down to the table where Grandpa Cliff carved turkey and swipe an early piece or two. In the spring, we'd practice for cheerleading tryouts.

All those years, we took the naked lady in the basement for granted.

But make no mistake, she was really something.

The naked lady adorned the plywood door of a built-in storage locker. She stood casually, almost life-size, a painted outline with wood-tone for flesh in front of maroon stage curtains. Her cheekbones were sculpted, and her coal black hair fell curly and long. Her lips were painted a dangerous red that matched the transparent, trailing scarf she draped above her head. The effect was old-fashioned, artistic, and maybe a touch sexy, if you were looking for that.

Stacy Liz and I weren't. She'd been born just a year after me, with a tangle of her own black hair, eyes that switched color, and freckles she never seemed thrilled about. She was spunky cuteness and lots of smarts. One day, she finally happened to ask, "What's that naked lady doing down here, anyhow?"

"Always has been," I said, like I was talking about tornadoes or prairie grass. "It's a good question, though."

Later on, back at home, I asked Mama about the naked lady and she simply exclaimed, "Cynthia Louise!" That was all Mama had to say on the subject.

At first, it didn't dawn on me to ask my grandparents. After all, grandparents were not people who I talked to about naked ladies. But it wasn't long before I spent a weekend at their house, like I did every couple of months. We lived in different suburbs of the Kansas City metro area, them in Raytown and me in Lenexa. No more than twenty minutes apart by car, but not walking distance. Just far enough that sleepovers seemed like a good idea.

That night, my parents slipped out at about eight-thirty, excusing themselves with the fact that Daddy had to open the Oldsmobile dealership in the morning and Mama wanted to be first in line at the Macy's white sale. Grandma Dottie said it was a sign of the times, how busy everyone was those days. Grandpa Cliff made some comment about the recession. I had faith in President Jimmy Carter, who reminded me of Mr. Rogers, what with his soft voice, button-up sweaters, and casual shoes.

Upstairs in the kitchen, Grandma Dottie was making a plate of snacks that would've made my mama fret about tummyaches—sour cream potato chips with icy Coke, some leftover Easter fudge, and a jar of roasted peanuts.

Downstairs in the basement, I watched Grandpa Cliff carve a bear out of a block of wood. He'd taken up carving not too long before, and on his workbench stood wooden eagles, deer, a cowboy hat, and the bust of a Mohawk man. He'd worked his whole life for the telephone company because it was a good steady job, but Grandpa loved carving.

That scene was typical of life as I understood it. I thought I knew my grandparents, their stories, and who they were. Grandma made snacks and talked up a storm. Grandpa's manner was quieter, an artist at heart.

Grandpa and I didn't always say much when we spent time together, but I never felt like there was a question I couldn't ask. After a while, I gestured to the naked lady. "Where did she come from?" I wanted to know.

"I painted her," he told me. "There's not much harder to paint than the human form, gettin' the proportions just right. She's a little short, don't you know, but not by too much." Grandpa Cliff kept on talking about painting and art. For all his talent, Grandpa never saw art as something to sell. He did it for the sake of doing it, and he spoke about that for quite a while.

I was happy to hear whatever he told me, even though it wasn't the answer I'd been after. But my mind wandered. Who was the naked lady? Someone he'd known long ago? Someone from his imagination? I studied the naked lady's womanly curves and dark, mysterious beauty. Would I look anything like that someday?

When it finally sounded like Grandpa's talk was running out, I still didn't get to ask the question. Grandma Dottie hollered down that snacks had long been ready, and so we ambled back upstairs. Grandpa Cliff skipped his snack and shuffled off to bed right away, tweaking my nose, and calling me Cindy Lou. Before long, his snores echoed through the two-bedroom house.

Luckily, Grandma Dottie was a night person like me. She settled in her recliner and lit up a cigarette. The snack tray sat on the coffee table. I could tell we'd be up pretty much the whole night, plenty of time to ask about the naked lady. I curled up on the sofa, waiting for the right moment.

To the outside world, Grandma was striking—amply busted with manicured nails and long, coal-black hair pinned in curls on the top of her head. She wore tailored pantsuits. Her only makeup was reddish lipstick. But Grandma looked like a totally different person in house clothes, in this case a daisy-print duster and terry-cloth slippers. The two of her features I'd inherited were a decent bustline and short arms. The way I had it figured, one made up for the other.

"So, tell me everything," Grandma Dottie said. "How's school?"

I nibbled on my potato chips and told her about my

handsome teacher, Mr. Rideout, who'd read us *Old Yeller*, which had made the meanest boy in class cry.

I talked about my grades. I confessed that I'd gotten 100 percent on a quiz about converting Fahrenheit to Celsius by sheer luck, an act of God, or some paranormal intervention. I'd completely guessed on every answer, using birth dates and my address and the number of students in my row.

I didn't have to worry about what she would think of that. Though she grew up Baptist and watched the Sunday morning services on TV, Grandma Dottie kept a large stack of *Fate* magazines by her desk, each filled with stories of extraterrestrials, psychics, Bigfoot, sorcerers, mummies, ghosts, near-death experiences, and the monster of Loch Ness. An astrology wheel—Grandma was a Virgo, Grandpa was a Leo—hung proudly above the guest towels on the bathroom wall.

Don't get me wrong. The house had its share of more mainstream belief systems. A Holy Bible, Living Bible, and Book of Mormon sat on the end table beside Grandpa's recliner, behind the candy dish shaped like a squirrel on a nut. A painting of Adam and Eve in the garden of Eden hung in the dining room.

Grandpa had grown up in the Reorganized Church of Jesus Christ of Latter-day Saints, but he went with Grandma Dottie to see famous psychics.

My grandparents were open-minded.

Despite that, I still couldn't tell Grandma Dottie about being a foot taller than everybody else in my grade, how a shrimpy boy called me Queen Kong, or, in the changing sands of sixth-grade society, how I couldn't seem to hang on to a best friend for more than a few months at a time. I couldn't tell her how a bully made fun of my T. J. Maxx red-dot clothes or how status was bought and sold with Gloria Vanderbilt jeans.

I didn't want to seem unhappy. Happiness was important to Grandma. Her tiny house was filled with bluebirds, hundreds of bluebird figurines in glass and porcelain and one bluebird music box that played "Close to You." They're symbols of happiness, and so I knew she wanted happiness all around. I asked her about it, wanting happiness. It was a question about Grandma herself, and she was more important than the naked lady.

"When I was a girl," she began, "things were all different. You're so lucky now, having your mama and daddy and everybody, who love you so much. When I was your age, my mama was dead and Daddy had remarried to start a new family." Grandma Dottie briefly disappeared into her bedroom and returned with a black-and-white photograph I'd seen before, hanging on the wall beside her antique dresser. "This was my mother," she said, handing it to me to study and then settling back in her chair.

The woman, Great-Grandma Mary Elizabeth, looked young, baby-faced almost, with dark eyes and hair. Glancing to my side, I caught a glimpse of my own reflection in the huge mirror above the sofa and realized that she'd looked a good bit like me. I wasn't much on my looks and found the resemblance something of a comfort.

My great-grandma had died at age thirty-two of what

was most likely sugar diabetes.

"That's why Daddy farmed out my sisters and me, sent us off to live with neighbors and relatives," Grandma Dottie explained, taking a drag on her cigarette. "Because Mama died, and he was too busy with his new family to take care of us."

It seemed to me that my great-grandfather had been wrong to put his new family so far ahead of his old one. But it also seemed disrespectful to say so, and I'd heard men and women were different back when.

I sipped my Coke and thought about Grandma Dottie as a young girl, practically orphaned. It was like learning about a completely different person, one who had nothing to do with being a grandma, wearing reddish lipstick, or making unhealthy snacks. By age thirteen, Grandma had been supporting herself.

"Now, don't look so long-faced," Grandma Dottie said. "I came out all right. When I was your age, I played tennis at the public park, went to the youth group activities at church, and hit the ten-cent movie once a week. Give me a candy bar for a nickel, and I was all set. They were silent movies, you know, and somebody played the piano. I'd go swimming, too. The boys swam one session, and the girls swam the other. And as I got a little older, well, back in those days, I wasn't bad looking. Back then, you could flatter a man and get anything you wanted and still do no wrong."

The buzzer sounded then, on the dryer down in the basement with the naked lady. Just when things were getting interesting. Of course, I'd known that Grandma Dottie had men in her life before my grandpa, but it was something new to hear her talk about it.

That girl who'd been farmed out, that young woman who'd relied on her looks, the elder who was confiding in me right then, none of them seemed like my old image of Grandma. I was starting to wonder how many people one woman could be.

It must be a sign of my growing up, I decided, that she was wanting to confide in me, to show me more of who she really was and had been.

"Come on, Cindy Lou," Grandma Dottie said, snuffing out her cigarette. "Let's see about my towels."

It was about a half hour after my bedtime. Grandma showed no signs of caring a lick, and I sure didn't mind. I followed her through the cramped dining room and thin, galley-style kitchen to the garage housing her black VW bug, and then down a set of creaky wooden stairs to the basement. The naked lady seemed to welcome us as we made our way into her domain.

Grandma Dottie headed toward the washer, dryer, and freezer that stood against the far wall, directly across from the naked lady. I followed, two steps back.

"What about your grandmas?" I asked. I'd been thinking about how Grandma Dottie and my great-aunties had been shipped off by their father. I knew that if anything ever happened to my parents, there would be family lining up to take care of me and that my grandparents would be first in line. So what if back then people saw raising kids as women's work? Shouldn't my grandma have had grandmas herself?

Grandma Dottie unloaded the dryer and began folding

bath towels. "I never knew my mother's mother," she said. "Daddy's mother, Grandma Walker, she didn't like kids."

The one light above us was just a bulb with a cord pull-string. It looked too bright in the dank basement.

"How can a grandma not like kids?" I asked, mystified.

Grandma Dottie shook her head. "Did I ever tell you," she asked, "that Grandma Walker had known the Jesse James gang?"

It's pretty much impossible to grow up in that part of the country and not know a thing or two about Jesse James. All along the Missouri highways, signs boasted of the places of his life and death. Jesse, his brother Frank, and their gang had been outlaws in the mid-to-late 1800s. Their legend got bigger than their real-life britches, mostly on account of the fact that Ozark folks admired their loyalty to the Old South.

"Grandma Walker was an orphan girl," Grandma Dottie explained, "and back then, the state would send orphan kids to work for farm families who'd give 'em room and board in return. The people she stayed with, they were big supporters of the gang. Those boys would ride into their barn, put up their horses, and then take a tunnel into the house. Your great-grandma, she'd have to wake up in the middle of the night and cook for them. People talk about those James men now, all romanticlike. But they were a rough crowd, and being around them, those murderers, affected her personality. It kind of closed her off inside." Grandma Dottie sounded serious and sad.

As I set the dryer timer, I realized then that part of Grandma Walker still lived in Grandma Dottie, just like part of each of them both would always live in me. I realized that so much of what made people who they were was cloaked in their pasts, in their family histories, in mystery. The naked lady drew my gaze again.

As Grandma Dottie lifted her arms to hang a silky blouse on the clothesline, I suddenly saw the resemblance. The curly, long, dark hair, now pinned up and tinged gray. The still-sculpted cheekbones, still dangerously red lips. "She's you!" I exclaimed, nodding toward the plywood door.

"Well, she was," Grandma Dottie said, chuckling softly. "But that was a long time ago. I posed—wearing shorts and a tank top, I'll have you know—for your grandpa."

"Why is it still in the basement?" I asked.

"I never thought about why," she said. "But it helps me remember when, I guess. I think I looked pretty darn good. Don't you?"

Grandma Dottie struck the pose—the naked lady one—and we laughed a good long while. I was seeing her, really seeing her. I saw her in the past and the present, and I saw myself carrying her memory into the future. She was some sexy grandma after all. It was funny, but I figured in a few years I just might be sexy, too. At least the part of me that was Grandma Dottie. The line wasn't a straight one, it looped back on itself, and it all seemed connected somehow.

As the history and future slipped back into shadows, Grandma Dottie winked at me, picked up the plastic laundry basket full of folded bath towels, and led me back up the creaky stairs. "The karma always catches up to you," she said. "Remember that."

♍

I took a couple of liberties in the writing of this story, crashing together a few events to help along the pacing and the flow. Besides which, Stacy Liz, being a whole lot brighter than I, probably figured out the relationship between our grandma and the naked lady long before I did. But the heart's just right, the balance of the love and the respect. That's what matters most.

At the time of this writing, Grandma Dottie, age eighty-three, still lives in her two-bedroom house in Raytown, Missouri. She's a widow now. My grandfather passed away from cancer two years ago, and losing him has been hard on all of us. But Grandma Dottie still dresses to kill, putters around in dusters, and tries to feed people silly. She gets her hair done once a week at the beauty shop, wears reddish lipstick, gambles with her friends on the Missouri River, and is proud to have been immortalized as the naked lady on the plywood door in her basement. Much of the best in me comes from her, and I'm grateful for it.

MINFONG HO

Rhizomes

How do I do this? I don't even know how to begin. She seems so far away and long ago. How can I reach her? I sit here at my desk, watching the pale morning sunlight filter through the green splinters of the bamboo I planted years ago, when we first moved into this big house in the middle of nowhere.

It's not really that *she* is far away, my grandmother, but that *I* have moved so far away from her, strayed way off-center, when I settled into this spot half a world away from where she used to live and where I grew up. My desk back home used to overlook rice fields edged by palm trees and water buffaloes wallowing in the mudholes. My grandmother's house, although it was a few hundred miles away, was in a similar setting, with the familiar sound of palm fronds and bamboo groves rustling in the tropical breezes or monsoon rains.

No monsoons here; no water buffaloes, either. Upstate New York is on the other side of the world from Thailand and Singapore, and the sounds and smells and sights that had seemed so much a part of me are now irretrievably distant.

But the bamboo I thought I could at least replicate, having found a hardy Northern variety that could withstand the fierce winters here. So I planted a small cluster of it outside my study window so that I could look up from my desk and see some familiar bamboo instead of the very big, very red, very American barn that's screened by it now.

This screen of bamboo helps, but not much. In the thick of winter, the snows often blanket the bamboo leaves so thickly that the thin stalks are bent over double under the weight of the snow. Sometimes I would have to wade through the knee-deep snow and shake loose the branches so that they could spring upright again.

It's pretty resilient stuff, bamboo—like Ah Po, my grand-mother. I miss her, of course. I miss feeling connected with my past, with people who knew me as a child and who can say my name the way it's supposed to be said: "Minnng-fong!" dragging out the first syllable, then with that tonal Cantonese lilt on the second. Over here, nobody sees the child I was in the adult that I am, and nobody says my name the way it's meant to be said. No wonder, then, that when the snow starts falling and the gray days stretch out before me, I feel so cut off from home.

I wonder if she felt as cut off from her home, after she left China and married my grandfather in Singapore. How did she communicate with the home she left behind? The postal service was erratic at best, especially after the Communist takeover of China in 1949 (and besides, she couldn't read or write), and the phone lines nonexistent.

Nor could she even return home for occasional visits. It

was so impossible to travel in those days that she couldn't even attend her mother's funeral.

Did you feel homesick too, Ah Po?

"Ah Po?"

"Ah Po." I said it aloud just now: "Ah Po," and yes, there you were.

How is it that just calling for you, quietly, expectantly, made it feel as if you were really nearby, within easy reach—upstairs, maybe, or out in the garden? Is it because it reminded me of the way you called for Ah Gung, my grandfather, when you wanted to talk to him, standing before his photograph in front of the ancestral altar?

"Ah Po." Yes, there you are.

It's as if the simple act of calling you had somehow collapsed the shadowy stretch of time and space, and of life and death, between us, and brought you right before me.

Did you call out to Ah Gung because that was the easiest, simplest, by far most direct way to keep connected?

I remember how you always talked to him, once all the offerings of food and wine and joss sticks had been arranged properly on the little wooden shelf. Standing there stiffly, you would give him updates on the state of the family, like some on-the-spot CNN reporter posed in front of the latest war zone.

"Our family is fine," you'd say, enunciating clearly. "Ah Wah, our eldest son, is visiting for Chinese New Year. See, here is Minfong, their eldest daughter." And you would prod me toward the altar.

"Greet him," you would say, with that tone of ironic

solemnity that you reserved for talking to the dead. "Greet your grandfather."

"Ah Gung," I would say, in the general direction of the altar, aiming somewhere a little higher than the black-and-white photograph of him. My grandfather stared down at me benignly.

"Light some incense for him." You would hand me three delicate joss sticks and dutifully I would lean over and light them from the tips of those burning in the brass bowl until tendrils of smoke curled up from mine as well.

"Now bow," you'd say. "Three times."

Joss sticks clasped between my palms, I would bow once, bow twice, bow three times—deeply, from the waist down. Then I would jab my joss sticks into the sandy ashes of the incense bowl.

"Now, this next one is Ah Wah's eldest son," you'd intone. "See what a fine boy he is?" And as my brother took his turn at the altar I would slip outside to play with my cousins and help them light strands of red firecrackers.

If only I had stayed behind, Ah Po, and listened more attentively, when you paid your respects to Grandfather in front of the altar. That sense of easy continuity between those in our family who died and those who were still alive is something I wish I was part of now, so that I could still feel as naturally connected to you, as you did to Grandfather. I know you had some special way of communicating with him, that sequence of rituals you used in front of the ancestral altar, your offering of joss sticks, the splashing of tiny porcelain cups of wine onto the floor, sometimes the folding and burning of paper "money" in the brazier.

Countless times I must have watched you doing it and taken part in it myself as well. How is it that I never learned how to do it on my own?

Instead I find myself fumbling when I try to talk to you now. How do I address you? What should I say? How many sticks of incense should I burn; how do I fold those horns of paper money to burn for you? I don't know how to set up any altar, and joss sticks aren't even available in the little Upstate New York town where I live.

I remember very vividly that last time you had me pray in front of the ancestral altar with you. You wanted to introduce John and me to Ah Gung as a couple about to be married. You brought us both to the altar, not insistently—no, you never did anything too insistently—and had us both bow with our lit joss sticks. It didn't seem to matter to you that John couldn't speak or understand Cantonese, nor that—as an American of Irish Catholic descent—he might worship other spirits in other ways.

"Here is Minfong and the man she is going to marry tomorrow," you told Ah Gung, or his spirit, or your memory of him—the distinctions didn't seem to matter. "She is all grown-up now and ready to start her own life with this man. He isn't Chinese, but he is kind and gentle, a good man, your son has told me that and I have seen it for myself." I liked the way you talked to him—conversationally, though a little louder than usual, as if Ah Gung might be deaf, or far away.

And the next day, the day of the wedding itself, you

presided over the Tea Ceremony with such aplomb. Dressed in your best "samfu" outfit, the loose high-collared shirt over equally loose pants of the same material, your hair neatly combed back behind your ears, a jade bracelet on your thin wrist, you sat on the high-backed mahogany chair as first I and then John served you tea. Do you remember how I, in my nervousness at being in front of so many wedding guests, invited you to drink your tea by saying only "Yum-chai, Ah Po," while John correctly recited "*Chang* yum-chai, Ah Po," saying, "*Please* drink the tea, Ah Po," rather than my abrupt "Drink the tea." Everyone burst out laughing, appreciative of John's more polite wording, and you beamed at him.

It was a form of playacting, this simple ceremony of serving tea to each relative or friend and having them drink the tea as their acceptance of our marriage. In the Chinese tradition, bowing to the ancestral altar was meant to include dead relatives as part of the extended family in the festivities.

I wonder what you thought of the Catholic wedding you attended later the same day, at St. Ignatius Church just down the road. You sat in the front row, the hum of the ceiling fans probably sounding more familiar to you than the drone of a language you did not understand, of concepts that I had tried, rather halfheartedly, to explain to you.

I remember how impossible it was for you to believe that newborn babies were imbued with original sin, that it took a painful sacrificial act to atone for this and redeem mankind. Accustomed as you were to the higher spirit—or, as the Chinese so simply refer to it, "Sky"—as being more benign, the whole idea of sacrifice seemed unnatural and, well, wasteful to you. Yes, you slaughtered plump white chickens and offered them all plucked, boiled, and glistening on porcelain platters in front of the ancestral altar, but that wasn't a sacrifice so much as a symbolic act, an attempt to feed loved ones in death, just as you did when they were alive. And besides, we always ate the chicken ourselves afterward. It went against the grain of your frugal, pragmatic Chinese soul to revere the concept of sacrifice, to glorify the inherent waste of it.

And so, even as I was walking down the aisle in my requisite white gown to the strains of the wedding march on the church organ, I was aware of your mild discomfort, that such an occasion for joy was taking place under the eyes of a life-size statue of the long-suffering Christ nailed to his cross. Did it help you, perhaps, to think of John and me as plump chickens being lovingly and symbolically offered up to Him?

What was your own marriage like, Ah Po? Did you and Ah Gung serve tea ceremonially as well, to his parents? Were your own parents there? Your father was living in Singapore, a well-to-do shipbuilder of fishing boats, but your mother—his first wife—hadn't she been left in China with you, while he started another household with a second wife? What was it like, growing up the uncherished daughter of a woman who had been displaced by a younger wife? Were you made to feel your parents' disappointment—that you had not been born a son? One of the few stories that you used to tell was of the time when you were fifteen years old and your mother had finally given birth to a second child—another girl!—while Second Wife had already borne two sons. Disgraced, your mother had been told (by your father? By your stepmother?) to eat in the kitchen instead of at the main dining table. She did, retreating quietly to sit in a corner of the dark kitchen, by the charcoal stove. Later you found her lying on her bed, eyes closed, dressed in her best clothes—and in a flash of dread and understanding, you reached under her pillow and grabbed the remaining opium pellets hidden there and took them away from her, aborting her attempted suicide. Even as an old woman, when you told the story you would have to wipe away tears from your eyes. Was she restored to her rightful place at the main table after that, Ah Po? Or did she climb out of her opium-induced grogginess only to sit in the kitchen corner, next to the charcoal stove?

I feel close to her, Ah Po, this great-grandmother whom I've never met. I would have liked to have seen her, touched her, known her. As it is, the closest I have ever come to her is to walk into her dim kitchen and touch the grimy wok on the charcoal stove that I think she used to cook at.

That was on my second trip to China, Ah Po, several years after you had already died. It was during Chinese New Year, and we were having a big family reunion in Canton. We counted up your progeny: seven children, thirty-eight grand-children, fifty-six great-grandchildren (too bad the handful of great-great-grandchildren that you have now were not born yet).

We had a family portrait taken, all together, all smiling

into the camera, almost as if we were posing to show ourselves to you: There, Ah Po, there's your family—all of us together!

The next day, we all piled into a chartered bus and made the trip—the pilgrimage, really, back to Sun Wuey, your hometown. Instead of the three days and two nights that you had described the trip taking, the bus took only two hours. Bridges and highways connected us to it, where before you had to take ferries and trucks and even oxcarts.

When we arrived in Sun Wuey, we found a modern, bustling city. We got off the bus and then threaded our way on foot, behind my father, through to an old, grimy section of town. Past flaking walls and down twisting alleyways we went in a long, straggling line over the paved stones.

I walked through the courtyard and into the little house adjacent to it. Mud walls, tiny windows with wooden shutters, dirt floors—there was a warren of small rooms that left no clear impression on me. Then I was in the kitchen, and there was a black wok resting on a charcoal brazier, its underside thickly encrusted with soot and grease. A square patch of light from the open window above fell on it. I reached out and touched the wok and felt a strange sense of vertigo, as if I was looking down a deep well of time. She might have held its handle countless times, my great-grandmother, as she stir-fried onions and tofu and peppers there, and you might have been right next to her, helping. I stroked the cold, smooth metal with my fingers, Ah Po, and felt that I had reached through time and made contact—actual, physical, tangible contact—with your own mother.

It was only natural that the dark little kitchen with its wok would be the link between the four generations of us women-folk. After all, so much of your life was spent cooking—as is mine, often against my will. Like you, I do all my own cooking for my family, three times a day, thirty days a month, twelve months of the year. It's not something that I am very skilled at or take particular pride in, but sometimes I do look at my growing children with satisfaction and think: Every ounce of flesh on those young bones has materialized out of the food that I cooked and fed them! Did you derive the same satisfaction from cooking? No wonder you used to pinch the chubby cheeks of your grandchildren!

I wish you had taught me to cook. Every time we came for a visit, there would be a banquet prepared. On feast days you would make elaborate dishes—shiitake mushrooms simmered in oyster sauce, crispy-skinned roast chicken, winter melon soup cooked right within the melon rind—but my favorites were the simple, quick meals you made: *mee-siam*, that spicy rice noodle dish flavored with lime juice and garnished with slices of hard-boiled eggs, which you used to slice with a piece of thread held taut between your hands.

Or steamed fish, placed neatly from head to tail on a long porcelain platter, and sprinkled with slivers of ginger and scallions, sometimes a handful of dried sour plums, and put in a woven bamboo steamer.

I did try to learn how to steam fish the way you did. Do you remember my asking you, "Ah Po, how long must you steam the fish for?"

You looked up from fanning the charcoal fire long enough to give me a puzzled look. "Until it's done, of course," you said.

Instead of *mee-siam* and steamed fish, I make spaghetti sauce and baked chicken. Sometimes, for variety, I will whip up some stir-fry, but it's generally something ad hoc, from whatever leftover vegetables are at the bottom of the fridge drawer—nothing elaborate, nothing you would enjoy eating.

How did you learn to cook, Ah Po? Had your own mother taught you, at that soot-encrusted wok in the dark kitchen back in China? Or did you learn more or less on your own, as a young wife, living in a new country that must have seemed strange and unfamiliar to you? Had you left your home reluctantly when you boarded a boat at seventeen to travel from southern China to Singapore, to your father's new home which he had set up with his second wife? Had your father sent for you, knowing that you were of marriageable age, so that he could arrange a match for you?

I know so little about your life as a young woman, Ah Po, and because I was so young and you seemed so old, I never thought to ask. I know that you got married at eighteen to a young carpenter, an apprentice boat-builder whom your father had matchmade you with. And within nine years, at age twenty-seven—the age at which I got married—you already had seven children. How on earth did you manage?

You lived for much of your married life in a two-room thatched hut at the edge of the sea, in a corner of the shipyard that Ah Gung worked in. Was the house built on stilts or right on the sand? There was a wooden boardwalk, extending out to the sea, that served as an outhouse for the family. I know that my father used to joke about how, as a little boy, he liked watching the fish gather as he defecated into the sea.

It could not have been easy, Ah Po. Two rooms, seven kids. How did you all fit in? The bedroom was for you and your five daughters, sleeping on rattan mats spread out at night, probably under mosquito nets, over the floor boards. The other room, which served as living room and dining room during the day, became the bedroom for Ah Gung and your two sons at night, as they unfolded canvas cots alongside one another.

"But then . . . if you and Ah Gung slept separately," I asked once, at a Sunday lunch where dozens of our family were gathered, "how did you produce so many children?"

There was a shocked silence. First Aunt and Second Aunt looked appalled. My father threw me one of those glowering "you've become too Westernized" looks. But you looked at me and said something vague like, "It happened." And then you smiled your toothless smile.

The aunts giggled. My cousin Ying Ying, wanting perhaps to be even more daring than I, said, "Maybe it happened while the kids were all at school."

"But I didn't go to school," First Aunt said. "Only the boys got to go."

More giggling. Second Aunt said, "We were told to go play outside."

The giggles became loud laughter, almost raucous. "But seven kids! That's so many to chase outside!"

"There weren't seven in the beginning. It must have been easier then . . ."

On and on it went, with my cousins teasing and daring one another to ask ever more suggestive questions, while our aunts laughed so hard that they were wiping tears from their eyes. And you looking on, the center and the point of origin for all this life and laughter, soaking it all in.

Do you remember, Ah Po, when you spoke my name that last time?

You were already hospitalized, lying there so thin and flat that you were like one of those paper cutout dolls, your gnarled hands protruding from the starched hospital gown. You had developed pneumonia from a persistent cough, and the family doctor had arranged for you to be hospitalized. While there, you contracted jaundice from some blood transfusion and weakened rapidly.

Eighty-four you were that year, and yet none of us were really prepared for the inevitable. For days we gathered around your hospital bed, in droves, all those relatives who are part of our family network. And, strange as it may seem, there was such a sense of strength, and yes, almost cheerfulness there, because of all the bustle of family around. Ping Ping was there, the little great-grandchild that you doted on, nicknamed "Hoi-sum goa"—Happiness Fruit—lithe and mischievous as always, scattering her lightheartedness around like pixie dust.

And of course the three grandchildren dearest to your heart, the ones you raised yourself when they were left orphaned at an early age.

On my last day there I approached you, and even when I was standing right next to you, holding your gnarled fingers in mine, you seemed remote, already quite far away. Your eyes were closed, your hair combed neatly back from your high forehead, your skin smooth and cool to the touch. And I didn't want to disturb you, thought perhaps you were beyond recognizing me anyway. But someone, Second Aunt perhaps, since she was always a bit bossy, someone pushed me from behind and urged me to call to you. And so I leaned forward and said, awkwardly, "Ah Po, how are you, Ah Po?"

Louder, Second Aunt said. So I said it again, more loudly, even more awkwardly, sure now that you couldn't really hear me or see me or know me.

Your eyelids fluttered open, and you took a deep breath. I saw your chest rise and fall under the blue gown, and you said, clearly, "Ming-foooong." From deep within your chest the sound came, so clearly, so definitively that I knew myself to be inextricably rooted to you.

I'm sorry I had to leave you shortly after that, Ah Po, with you lying there so frail and weak, but my aunt in California was in the terminal stages of cancer, and my mother was too much of a dutiful daughter-in-law to leave you, so she sent me in her stead.

En route from Singapore to California, in the transit

lounge in Honolulu, I called relatives in San Francisco to see how my aunt was doing and learned that she had just died. I then called Singapore, to find out how you were, and was told that you, too, had died.

The rest of that trip was a total blur, as were the days that followed. I attended my aunt's funeral, but I wasn't there for yours, Ah Po, and I'm sorry.

When I got back "home," to that cramped apartment that John and I rented from the university, I slipped back into the rut of student life: went to classes, did research in the library, wrote term papers.

It was not until fall was almost over and the trees half bare that I gave way to a wave of panic at the approaching winter. I hate the winters here, Ah Po—it is like nothing you have ever experienced or that I will ever get used to. The snow falls in November and doesn't melt until April. The six long months in between are such a dreary tunnel of gray and brown that you almost forget what the color green looks like. I had always dreaded the coming of winter, but that fall, after you died, the dread was close to a panic. I felt as if I literally could not make it through to spring.

On an impulse, I bought a handful of daffodil bulbs and planted them in a clearing in the woods near where I lived. A semicircle of five bulbs around one in the center, our little nuclear family revolving around you. I also planted a birdnest pine there, simply because I liked its name. After all, what I wanted, and was trying to create, was a sense of a nest—an evergreen one, no less.

Through that fall and that winter, I kept going back to that clearing—sprinkling bonemeal to fertilize the bulbs, brushing the snow off the birdnest pine, or just sitting quietly on the log nearby.

Finally, eight months after you had died, the deep snows melted and the ground started to thaw. In the early spring I made my way back through the winding path, half hidden by bramble, into the clearing.

And there they were—the daffodils, six of them, poking out from the mat of sodden maple leaves, like droplets from the bright spring sun. I knelt there and scooped handfuls of old leaves away until the stalks rose free and tall from the cleared ground and the blossoms danced in the breeze.

And watching them, I broke down and wept, because they had made it through the winter, these daffodils, but I still missed you.

I miss you even now, Ah Po, so many years later. I have settled here, just a few miles from the cluster of those daffodils I planted in your memory. And in the years since then, I have planted willows and evergreens, pear trees and juniper, wide patches of peonies and Siberian irises. Climbing roses and wisteria vines too, we have planted—John and I—and he has built wooden trellises along the house for them. I wish you could see my garden in the spring, Ah Po, you would take such delight in the profusion of colors and smells. And of course there is the bamboo, growing exuberantly outside my study window.

I have three children, Ah Po, all of them healthy and happy. I wish that you could have seen them and held them in your arms, the way you must have held me when I was a baby left in your care. And though I doubt that I will ever get organized enough to have each of them pay their respects to you in front of some altar, bowing with joss sticks in their hands, often when I look at them I think of you and present them to you silently: Here, Ah Po, is Danfung, and Meimei, and Chris—your great-grandchildren.

You have so many great-grandchildren now, Ah Po—not just mine but my brother's, and my cousins'. You even have great-great-grandchildren, Ah Po. The last time I went back home to Singapore for Chinese New Year, I held a very special new baby in my arms: He was the grandchild of my cousin Ah Sien, your oldest grandchild. So that made me a grand-aunt, I was told, and we all laughed at how we had been bumped up one generation by this baby's arrival, including even his little "uncle" Chuen-Chuen, who was just a toddler himself.

We still have the New Year reunion dinner at our house, Ah Po, just like we did when you were alive. There seems to be just the same mix of babies and teenagers and middle-age parents and old folks, except that, like everyone else, I have moved through the ranks from one age-group to the next. And though the three generations of your descendants are dispersed far and wide, throughout the U.S. and Canada and France and China and Thailand, we all try to come back for the reunion dinner when we can, to acknowledge that we are still connected to one another and, yes, to you.

Like bamboo shoots we are, Ah Po, sprouting out all around the original clump of bamboo. Just this spring, I noticed how there were tiny green shoots appearing ten, twenty feet from the central bamboo, so far away that it didn't seem like they were connected to the original growth at all. How did they get there? Did the bamboo have spores that were dispersed by the wind? Or seeds or nuts that birds carried off? How did these tiny shoots sprout so far away from the original plant? I asked John—who, after all, had grown up on a farm (and has a Ph.D. in agronomy).

"Rhizomes," he said.

Rhizomes, *Taylor's Encyclopedia of Gardening* explained, are underground roots that bear buds from which new shoots grow. Bamboos, it further explained, are woody-stemmed grasses that have long, thin rhizomes that grow quickly to varying distances from the mother plant before sending up new shoots.

Of course, I thought. And suddenly I understood how it was that we were all still so connected to you, Ah Po. Like those unseen rhizomes buried underground, you extend your memories, your genes, your love through time and space to connect us all to one another and to you. Intangible though they are, these spiritual and emotional rhizomes give me strength, Ah Po, and—no matter how far away and cut off I may sometimes feel—they connect me with a sense of family and with you.

Ah Po, this is a strange way of talking to you, I know—

without joss sticks, without bowing, without even speaking Cantonese. But this is the only way I know how to talk to you. Please, Ah Po, accept these clumsy English words as a silent offering from my heart, connecting me back to you.

AUTHOR'S NOTE

When I was a little girl growing up in Bangkok, there were two situations in which I would witness adults talking loudly and solemnly to people I couldn't see. One was when my father spoke on the phone long-distance to his business colleagues. The other was when my grandmother spoke to the spirits of her dead husband and various ancestors at the family altar. I came to regard both acts as natural forms of adult communication, one reaching through distance, the other through death.

After all, distance and death are just different degrees of separation, especially to a child of immigrants. As an immigrant myself, geographical distance can often feel as permanent as death. When we leave our homeland, putting a great distance between ourselves and those we leave behind, it can feel almost like a form of dying, because we know that we may never return again. Unlike those for whom travel means the luxury of a round-trip ticket, we immigrants often feel that leaving a place or a person can be as irrevocable as burning a bridge behind us. As in death, there is no going back.

When my mother said good-bye to her mother in Shanghai in 1936, she did not know that three wars and as many decades would go by before they would meet again, or that the meeting would be their last one. After that brief reunion, my grandmother returned to China and died there years later, without ever seeing her daughter again. That second leave-taking between mother and daughter must have been a truly heart-wrenching one, with both of them knowing that the distance between them would ultimately crystallize into death.

In much the same way, my paternal grandmother left China not knowing if she would ever see her mother again. She settled in Singapore, and eventually became the matriarch of a large extended family of seven children and countless grandchildren, but she never managed to see her own mother again—not even to attend her funeral.

Yet, through the years, all the members of my family have tried to stay connected despite being separated by distance or death. We have sent letters and telegrams, made phone calls, and passed on messages by word of mouth to those far away. Or we have lit joss sticks and offered food and tiny cups of wine at the altar of those who have died. Whether or not our messages get through is secondary. What remains critical is the understanding that it is this very process of trying to communicate with those we love and respect that binds us closer together and connects us as a family.

Until I wrote this essay to and for my grandmother, I

had not truly reached this understanding. I know now, though, that like the bamboo shoots sprouting around the little thicket outside my window, I am connected to my family by the intangible rhizomes of love.

PAT CUMMINGS

The Grannies

Grandmotherwise, I've been lucky. I got the sensible-shoed, silver-haired, ample-bosomed, candy-jar-on-the-coffee-table women who worked hard and made clear their devotion to their families. They both wore dresses at home! Fried food! Kept ladylike gloves in their top dresser drawer! They even filled pantries with cans and boxes whose contents could be whipped into dinners for six. I saw them do it. And, most importantly, they doled out the kind of unconditional love that, to this day, buffers me against any slings and arrows in my path.

My grandmothers fit the classic grandmother profile I found in the stories I read or the television shows and movies I saw as a kid: They were tough cookies but big softies. They didn't, on the surface anyway, resemble any grandmothers I know now who book vacations with frequent-flyer miles, twist themselves into yogic asanas, and slip out of their Nikes and into svelte Bruno Maglis for theater and lunch dates. The friends who show me pictures of their grandkids these days are friends who take continuing ed classes, drive snazzy imported cars, and block out time on their PalmPilots for facials and manicures. Not a silver bun in the bunch.

I suspect grandmothers will always be wells of unconditional love, always be fonts of wisdom and guardians of tradition. Some things never change. A lot of my memories of my grandmothers involve food, however, so I'm glad I got the cookie-baking, deep-frying, snack-friendly treatment from them before everyone got so nervous about sugar and cholesterol. Being indulged senseless was a big part of being a grandchild when I was little.

Granny Cummings and Granny Taylor both lived in Chicago, Illinois. My mom and dad had been born and raised there, fallen in love and married there. I was born there, too. But my two sisters and brother and I grew up as army brats, moving around the planet every two or three years. The only spot on the globe to which we returned with any regularity was Chicago. We occasionally had the treat of visiting for Thanksgiving or Christmas but, without fail, every summer spent Stateside included an extended trip home.

Granny and Papa Cummings lived on a tree-lined residential street called South May. For a city home, it had a nice country feeling. There were lace doilies on the arms of Granny's chairs, and her living room, lit with sunlight and polished glass, gently eased us into her quiet, calm, orderly world. The front porch was just right for sitting and the backyard was perfect for any game we knew or could invent—if we could find the time.

Granny Cummings was a large, soft woman whose

nickname was Sweet. And she was. She was gentle and warm and laughed readily. Her hair was usually braided up neatly in a Heidi-like style or pulled into a coiled bun at the nape of her neck. Every dress she wore was pastel, shirtwaisted, and soft. That first hug coming through the door was scented with laundry and powder and whatever was cooking on the stove. After being squeezed senseless and examined head to toe, almost from the minute we arrived, there would be stuff for us to do. Time was a valuable commodity and Granny Cummings did not like to see it wasted. Fortunately, drawing at the desk in her dining room counted as being busy. There was a steady supply of paper and pencils to be found in that desk and as long as I was occupied, it was fine with her. I have no idea what it was that I was drawing but the fact that she took it seriously made art seem important. Granny considered it "work."

Across town on East 57th Street, Granny and Papa Taylor had a desk full of drawing paper as well. They lived in an apartment building with a small balcony in the front and a big yard in the back that we rarely visited. The front lobby in their building always smelled like a Sunday supper that included cabbage. I couldn't pin the aroma down to any door or even a particular floor, but the minute you pushed through the old, cut-glass door in the lobby, it hit you. My sister Linda and I would climb to Granny's second-floor apartment, drop our things on the huge twin beds waiting for us, and enter a no-rules zone. I could draw until my fingers fell off.

The desk at Granny Taylor's was between the balcony door

and her old black-and-white television set. So I missed nothing while I drew. And nothing was off-limits in those desk drawers, not the graph paper or the fragile sheets of onionskin paper, not the fountain pens or the mechanical pencils with their slender, breakable leads. Each drawer held a surprise: tiny scissors with a bird carved into the handle in one, in another a curious three-sided ruler that my grandfather used for his contracting business. Pure luxury.

There was no particular bedtime, and having dessert before dinner was okay. Granny Taylor let us douse chocolate ice cream with Hershey's syrup—surely the gold standard of decadence. Granny often unfolded a bed in the living room so Linda and I could watch the Late-Night Movie, the Late-Late-Night Movie, and the cartoons that signaled the end of the day's programming. Only after the last "Th-Th-That's all, folks," sputtered out of Porky's mouth did I close my eyes.

We couldn't get away with that at Granny Cummings's house. We went to bed early and piled into foldaway beds grumbling that we weren't tired. Then, straining to hear the grown-ups' conversations, we would drop off to sleep promptly. In the morning, Granny would take Linda and me along on her errands or on shopping trips to the A&P. We helped fill her cart, then pulled it home to unload bags of groceries. We'd set tables, clear dishes, make beds, scrub sinks and tubs, and, somehow, still find a bit of time to hang out under the tree in the backyard. Granny took a lot of pride in her house, and some little thing, somewhere, always needed to be cleaned or polished or tossed out. The chore that topped my list was getting to wash, dry, or put away the glossy little teacups and saucers that she kept stacked in her kitchen cupboard. The dishes were all lovely and delicate and included cheerfully mismatched stragglers from long-lost sets. That collection of dishes begged for a proper party. Every once in a while, usually when our cousins came over, we carefully laid out the cups and saucers for tea and got downright dainty. Linda collects teapots now, and no doubt that cupboard has something to do with it, but neither of us knows what became of Granny Cummings's dishes.

We went on shopping trips with Granny Taylor as well. Usually, that meant hopping on the El for a flying train ride out over the neighborhood rooftops. At least once during every visit Linda and I would zigzag alongside Granny, in and out of massive department stores in the Loop, Chicago's downtown area. We hopped onto sleek escalators under glittering chandeliers or boarded Art Deco elevators where men in snappy uniforms recited lyrical lists of departments: *"men's . . . misses' . . . ladies' lingerie."* Light bounced off mirrored surfaces, and trays of jewelry and scarves, trapped under glass counters, beckoned. Rows of chocolates and brightly colored marzipan candies were lined up right out in the open! Stuff, stuff, and more stuff. Marshall Field's. Carson Pirie Scott. Glitzy, gaudy stores that were over-the-top and perfect. They could not possibly have been as breathtakingly sparkly as I remember them.

I don't know how Granny withstood such visual bombardment, but by the time we headed home, Linda and I were still wired. Under the tracks of the El were newsstands with racks of comic books and Granny let us choose several apiece. Katy Keene, Brenda Starr, Superman, Archie and Veronica. I have known great wealth. When we were done with the intense selection process, we toted our shopping bags up stairways to the El and rode back to Granny's in ecstasy. Home at last, I would make a beeline for my bed to spread my treasures out: so many comics to read, so many paper doll books that all of the costumes couldn't be cut out in one sitting. *Abundance* is the word that comes to mind, but there was more. In one of her dresser drawers, Granny kept a can full of enameled, wooden, gilded, or glass buttons that needed to be strung into bracelets and paired into earrings. I could barely get my paper doll work out of the way with that kind of pressure looming.

As Linda and I bounced back and forth between grannies, we were blissfully unaware of the logistics and politics involved in dividing our time among the relatives. We were disciplined and calm at Granny Cummings's, where we sat down to family meals; at Granny Taylor's we were giddy night owls who ate pretty much as we pleased. The biggest difference was apparent in how we spent Sundays.

At Granny Cummings's house, we were up early, dressed and out the door for a morning in church. She was an exceptionally devout woman and we were raised as Catholics, went to catechism classes, sang in church choirs, took Communion, and said our prayers nightly. My sister Linda and I sprinkled our beds with holy water and confessed our sins quickly, not wanting to be run down by a speeding car before we had the chance to wash away our week's worth of venial sins. I honed my Catholic sense of guilt on Granny Cummings's time. If

I forgot and accidentally chewed the wafer (the body of Christ!)
I could find myself sinning even as I took Communion.
There was a lot to worry about.

By ushering us through all of the church rituals, I think
Granny Cummings hoped that faith would take root in us.
But religion stuck to me in bits and pieces. The Latin Mass
was intoxicating *because* I didn't understand a word of it.
The rituals seemed made of the same stuff as the spells and
incantations in my favorite books. And when the priest called
out "Et cum spiritu tuo," it was as if the gospel was giving
us God's home phone number: Ecum Spirit 2-2-0.

Over at Granny Taylor's apartment, Sunday was a big day
for church too. I have no memory of ever actually walking into
one with her but we had our Sunday ritual as well. Granny's
apartment was directly across the street from a wonderful
stone church. We didn't have to wake up early. We could wear
our pajamas. Watching the congregation from the couch was
more discreet but out on the balcony we had a better view.
It was Granny Taylor who taught Linda and me how to work
binoculars. We leaned, but not too far, over her balcony wall
for a slugfest of snooping on the devout, well-dressed crowd
that filled the doorway across the street every hour on the
hour. Granny was a snazzy dresser, and getting an extreme,
close-up inspection of the fox stoles and fancy hats, the chif-
fon, brocade, and fur on the faithful seemed to be as enter-
taining to her as it was to us. And somehow, Granny would
have whipped up her killer macaroni and cheese, baked a
ham, and fixed stringbeans and potatoes in between the comings and goings over at the church. When the urge hit us,

we ate. Sunday was for relaxing.

Holiday dinners at home were Granny Cummings's forte. She'd have started cooking by the time we kids woke up, and heady aromas would fill the house by midmorning. At suppertime, a leaf or two would have been added to the dining-room table, and there'd be a steady rotation of bowls and platters from aunt to niece, from mother to grandfather. A line leading into the kitchen was our only warning that a fresh batch of biscuits was coming out of the oven. And even the oldest uncle could get busted by the youngest grandchild if he was caught hogging them. There were never enough of Granny's biscuits and no such thing as leftovers. Things could get ugly if they simply ran low.

Somehow, in my mind, being able to cook got tied up with being able to reproduce those biscuits. Folded pillows of soft dough, each buttered on top repeatedly while baking, cooked until they were a golden brown. Time, it turns out, cannot dispel their aroma because I can smell them at will. I attempted to copy Granny's recipe only once, when I was in college. Not wise. The gnarled bread sticks I pulled from the oven that Thanksgiving weren't allowed at the table. No butter could permeate them. No knife could cut them. No tooth could gnaw them. I have been recipe-impaired ever since. Some disappointments can't be overcome.

Granny Taylor had a hairdressing business in her apartment and, during the week, her customers stopped by. She had a special chair that she pulled into the bathroom whenever it was time to shampoo our hair. Like she did with her customers, she would test the water's temperature before running her spray nozzle up and around, under the back of our heads to rinse out all of the suds. It felt heavenly. Her own silver hair she kept short. After she washed it, she showed Linda and me how she would style it: combing it straight back while wet, then pushing it here and nudging it there with her fingers, leaving elegant waves to simply dry in place.

Across town, when Granny Cummings washed her hair, it was an event. Sometimes she let me help unbraid it. And that hair was wild. In almost every picture I've seen of her, it is pinned down—if not tamed, at least restrained. Once I was sure that I had pulled out all of the hairpins (and she had run a hand over her head, double-checking my work) I could begin the unbraiding. It was shocking how long her hair was. That she could braid it up and tuck such a wild stream of silver into a tidy coil really intrigued me.

Visually, her hair was quite provocative. I didn't mess around with metaphors back then, never saw her hair as some crowning emblem of feminine beauty that she kept private. It just fascinated me. Like watching something hatch or looking at an eclipse of the moon in progress, I just appreciated that moment of transformation, from order to mayhem, as though it was a very cool trick she was willing to share, however sparingly.

Now, when her eye catches mine as I flip through a photo album, I suddenly remember sitting by her back then, leaning on the rim of her lion-footed bathtub and watching the way she worked the soap through her hair. The dark circles under her eyes are mine finally, just part of a blurring that I notice has begun. Little by little I've been growing into her body apparently. In so many ways, my face has become quite like hers. But I'll never have that hair.

Over the years, through the turbulent sixties and the revolution of the seventies, my grandmothers stayed constant. Whether I showed up Black and militant, slightly hippie, or in a dashiki, quite Afrocentric with my head wrapped in a gele, the world in my grandmothers' homes never seemed to change. Linda and I learned how to dance the Madison in Granny Cummings's basement, and Granny Taylor taught us the twist in her living room. "Just bend one knee forward and the other one backward," she urged, with one eye glued to the writhing couples on *American Bandstand*. The show would be over before we did any real damage.

Granny Cummings died in 1969, just as my college campus was erupting with protests against everything that smacked of being the "Establishment." All around me, students were working overtime to distance themselves from their parents' and their grandparents' generations. Anarchy was cool; anyone over thirty was the enemy. But I could never be part of that aspect of the revolution, because I had little to fight against on that score. Granny Cummings might have clucked over my army-navy jacket and frayed bell bottoms, but as long as I didn't try to wear them to church with her, I could wear what I wanted.

Granny Taylor lived longer and weathered her own share of changes. In the seventies, her seasoned fingers would comb through my Afro, itching for me to let her "do something with that hair." After I read *Roots*, she patiently let me interview her for posterity and grinned if I levitated when she used the words *Colored* or *Negro* in my progressive presence. She tolerated lengthy discussions of everything from the government's role in Vietnam to how Sly Stone's drug use was affecting his music. Neither grandmother quibbled about the trends we all dragged them through. Both seemed to hold themselves steady in some time period from their past, content with their own values but never insisting we share them.

I can see them change through the years in their pictures, of course. Most of the family photos are at my mother's house, and we all pull them out during visits. We fuss about who made off with which original or chide my mom about the lack of chronological order in her albums as we bounce back and forth through time. My grandmothers will continue to smile forever in them. In older photos they are stylishly dressed, their hair smartly coifed, wearing pumps and matching handbags, at times leaning on the arms of their dapper husbands. In some shots, their friends surround them, and I get a weird glimpse into their lives as someone's friend or classmate, a peek at the world they existed in before I knew them. Later, in photos where my brother and sisters and I begin to show up, they are the large, soft, crinkly women whom I have suspended in amber in my mind's eye. If it is a selfish, child's-eye view, it is, nevertheless, who they remain for me, my "real" grandmothers. And this is the first sensation that washes over me when I think of either of them: being gathered tenderly toward them for a good long hug.

After that, if I spend too long with the photo albums, I can't help but see them through the lens I use now. My grandmothers lived through blatantly racist times and experiences that seemed not to have left them embittered. Lucy Deruisa Cummings and Emma Marie Ewing Taylor lived hard lives. They worked all the time and didn't fuss about it. They just got on with it. They were family-first women who lived their lives as sisters and daughters, then as wives and mothers. Did they have aspirations that went unsatisfied? Could they have possibly been content to wait on their husbands and children? Did they have talents that were never encouraged or dreams that never materialized? They must have. If they felt limited by their sex or their race, their family responsibilities or their economic states, I was as unaware of it as a child as I feel sure of it today.

So, here's what I've decided happens: Eventually, with a bit of luck, you reach your grandmother's age. You look in the mirror and you see the spot you saw on her face, or the line at the corner of your mouth that is just like hers. And, sure enough, whenever I study their photos now, I'm starting to see myself. As late as it is, which is too late, I find myself wishing that these women whom I so clearly came from had had the gentler life they helped me have. That desire, retroactive and pointless, leaves a dull, radiating ache in my chest whenever I let my mind go down that path. I can't indulge them, now that I finally understand that they may have enjoyed a bit of indulgence. I can't lavish on them what they lavished on others. They gave a lot. I took a lot. Some things they handed over, some things I inherited. And some things seeped in just from being in the room while they talked.

I sometimes feel my grandmothers with me still. Occasionally in dreams. Oddly enough, in patches of sunlight. In memories that spring up while I'm sitting at my drawing table or walking down a tree-lined street. I have no idea why these memories come when they do. And certainly, a whiff of any dish either one of them used to cook can propel me right back to their kitchens in Chicago. Diet gurus might preach that my Pavlovian buttons need to be disconnected—but disconnect the aroma of macaroni and cheese, biscuits and pies, and potato salad?

Whenever I feel as though my footsteps are getting erased or the story of my family is growing hazy only a few decades behind me, any small reminder of my grandmothers' faith and humor can lift me up. Once, at a salon, my hairdresser Mykel told me, apropos of nothing, that my grandmother was there with me. He had always been psychic, he told me, but usually he preferred to ignore all of the spirits he saw drifting around the living.

"Over your shoulder," he said casually. "Her name starts with an 'M.,' right? She came in with you." I felt a warm chill—if there is such a thing—but actually, it didn't surprise me. Granny Taylor had always fussed over my hair and it made sense that she'd show up at the salon. The hairdresser changed the subject—he'd gone on to the latest book he was reading—but I wasn't paying attention. I was eighteen again, listening to Granny Taylor insist, "Let me do something with that hair."

AUTHOR'S NOTE

Memory has always been a funny thing for me, not especially linear but often intense. I know some people can recall chronological facts, but my memories just shiver in and out of my mind, triggered by sights, smells, and sounds. It's like thinking in watercolors. I might hear the scrape of a porch door or suddenly see the view from my grandmother's bedroom window in Chicago, circa the fifties.

Spending time thinking about my grandmothers brings them close to me once again. I'm fortunate. I get to write and illustrate stories that let me preserve bits of my family lore. In a book, I can share the warmth and security that my family gave me, that they still give me, with children who are in the middle of their own stories. I can change events to suit myself but I can't change the past, not a single hard time that my grandmothers experienced.

The truth is, I don't know that either of them would have done anything differently. Their histories shaped them just like they helped shape me. My grandmothers always seemed to be happy, positive women who showered my brother and sisters and me with unconditional love. They tried to give us the best of themselves. When you're little, you don't realize how rare a thing that is. When you're older, you find out how tough it is to be uncritical, to just love.

So, I send up a prayer. I send up my love. And I feel lighter. I try to keep Granny Cummings and Granny Taylor in mind, try to focus on all of the folks there are left to love and indulge. Just thinking about them makes me want to do something for someone else. What a gift that was to have left me! Somewhere, I trust the grannies are smiling.

The Doctor's Daughter

In 1976, my grandmother was eighty years old, newly widowed, and going blind from macular degeneration. Her active years were coming to a close, and she grew depressed and bitter at the turn her once-rich life was taking. Yet she would not go gentle into that good night. In one final burst of energy, she built a stone wall in the back of her house, visited India, and wrote her memoirs.

Then she began a rapid decline, physically and mentally. The last afternoon we spent together was in the summer of 1981, shortly before she died. She had suffered a series of small strokes and had forgotten, as a result, that she smoked. She knew she craved something. As we talked, her hands moved restlessly as if she were trying to recall what it was she needed to do with them. I'm not sure she knew who I was, and our conversation was disjointed. Still, even in disarray, hers was an interesting mind. What she wanted to know that afternoon was who had been president of Egypt in 1956—was it Nasser? I didn't have a clue, but I looked it up later, and it was.

Pearl Bunkley Grissom, mother of my mother, was the

matriarch of a creative and mildly eccentric family. She made no particular effort to call attention to herself or be at the center of things—she just was. She drew people to her with her easy manner and quick mind. It was not so much that Pearl was sweet; often she was blunt spoken and opinionated. But the thing was, she was fascinating. I remember a quote from *Auntie Mame*: "Life is a banquet and most poor suckers are starving to death." Not Pearl—she was the founder of the feast. She had been places and done things. She was interested in everything, and if you wanted to hear about it, she was happy to share what she knew.

Pearl was a natural storyteller, with a beautiful deep voice and a way with words. We were all spellbound by the tales of her childhood, and people were always telling her she ought to be a writer. She would dismiss the idea by insisting she had nothing important to say.

Then, in her eightieth year, she sat down to write a few of those stories she had told us so often—and she simply couldn't stop. When her handwritten notes were transcribed, they went on for sixty-seven typewritten pages, single-spaced. After the manuscript was copied and distributed to the relatives, Pearl remembered more things she wanted to include. Tucked in with my copy of the manuscript are ten pages torn from a spiral stenographer's notebook, written in a bold hand with a black felt-tip pen. The subject of her "last words" was suitably quirky and unexpected: "About Chickens and Turkeys."

Reading those pages now, so many years later, I am once again a child, playing with my grandmother's hair while she talks in that soothing voice about growing up in the Wild West.

She called them her "little girl stories," and they always began with her birth, in Anson, Texas, on November 5, 1896. Her father was the town doctor—in fact, the only doctor for many miles around. This was a good thing, because Pearl might not otherwise have survived.

"Two tumors lay in the womb with me," she wrote. "A small one pressed on the crown of my head, and a larger one lay against my chest. I was born prematurely and weighed three and a half pounds. There was no hospital nearer than Fort Worth and, of course, no incubator. Papa took a box and swaddled me well and laid me in it, and put it on the door of the kitchen range. And there I stayed for more than a month.

"The range was a wood-burner, and the door was hinged at the bottom so that when opened it made a kind of shelf. I slept most of the time for more than a month, and it was with great difficulty that I could be awakened enough to nurse.

"The tumors had left a sunken place in my skull, traces of which are yet discernable, and a much larger place in my chest. This one I came to feel was a mark of great distinction, as so many people seemed to want to lay their fists in it, if not to see it. I spoke of it as 'my hole,' to Mother's great chagrin.

"As soon as I was large enough to handle well, Papa began to exercise me, working my little arms back and forth, up and down. When I was still too young for school, Papa bought me a pair of tiny dumbbells. They were made of some hard wood and beautifully shined and finished. I stood by the hour, lifting them above my head in front of me, up, down and—the most difficult of all—clicking them together behind my back. . . . They made very satisfactory hollow sounds when they came together with force.

"As I grew, new, larger, and heavier dumbbells appeared, and finally, a woman who taught physical culture came to oversee my work with them.

"Papa also invented a kind of harness, which he got Mother to make for me, to hold my shoulders back. It was uncomfortable and humiliating. It had some kind of buckle in the back to draw it tighter. It took me long months to learn how to get out of it and into it again, but I finally did. When I started to school, I would go into the cloakroom, take that hated thing off and, before going home, put it on again. This was just wonderful until one day I forgot and left it in the cloakroom. I can still remember how hard I tried to make up a believable tale about how it had happened. I was cut short by Mother, who marched me right back to school and ordered me to demonstrate how I did it. Then she made some adjustments in the design, and I was never again able to shed it."

Pearl was full of personality from the get-go, and she was always in trouble—forever getting into fights or running away. She described herself, quite unashamedly, as "a fighter, a bully, and a liar. I lied about my age, my size, my weight, and the size of my shoes. I fought anyone who came around, using teeth, feet, hands, or any instrument that came to hand."

Pearl's mother was in "delicate" health and had four children to care for and a house to run. Dr. Bunkley must have decided that the most helpful thing he could do was to take Pearl off his wife's hands as often as possible. So from the time Pearl was four, he began taking her with him wherever he went.

"Papa would be called to some ranch," she wrote. "While we were there, a cowboy would come riding in with a message, and off we would go to another ranch after changing horses. We would often be gone for several days on these trips."

Whenever he had to get out of the buggy to open a gate, he would let Pearl hold the reins. For a four-year-old girl, that was grander than grand! When the weather was cold, he would bundle her up in a bearskin coat, hat, and gloves. Then he would wrap her in buffalo hides. On the floor of the buggy he kept a charcoal-burning foot warmer. As they rode along, Papa would tell her stories, demonstrate his skill with the buggy whip (in summer he could pop the heads off sunflowers), and explain the world.

When they arrived at a ranch house, Papa would go inside with his black doctor's bag tucked under his arm. "Inside the bag were several rows of glass bottles, each with a different medicine. A little trapdoor on one side held a small square of marble, a palette knife, and prescription blanks. It was kind of a traveling drugstore.

"Papa would put his marble palette on a table, open several bottles, then scoop out the contents with his palette knife. He would mix the powders carefully and measure out doses onto small squares of paper. Then he would fold each one into a little package, tucking the ends up carefully. He would write out instructions on a prescription blank.

"If his patient was a child, he would say, 'These don't taste bad. Pearl takes them. Here, daughter, show them how to take the medicine.' Proudly, I would stick my tongue way out and he would tap the powder onto the back of my tongue. It was years before I caught on to the fact that I, too, was being doctored. I only knew it gave me a chance to show how big and brave I was."

Pearl loved her father's office, and many days, after school, she would go there. "He had one chair such as dentists use, and also a tall stool, where I always sat. I was enchanted by his skeleton, which he kept in a tall case. Sometimes, in talking to a patient, he would open the door and point out just where the trouble lay. He taught me the names of all the bones in the body, and I could rattle them off like reciting a poem, even those little devilish ones in the hands and feet. As I said them, he had me point to the part of the body indicated. My favorite was 'medulla oblongata.' . . . I just loved the sound of it."

Pearl's stories were rarely dramatic—though one featured a cattle rustler and another a needle-grass storm—but they were fascinating to me because she managed to build, detail by detail, a vivid picture of a vanished world. She made me see their parlor with the green wallpaper, the family album and chocolate set arranged carefully on the round center table. A salesman is at the door offering new slides for the stereoscope, with pictures of disasters like the San Francisco fire. Soon ladies will come calling in their best hats. I can picture Pearl stealing cream from the butter churn or having her hair frizzed with the curling irons that were warmed in the chimney of a kerosene lamp. All of it became real to me, though it had happened half a century before.

By the time Pearl started telling these stories to her grandchildren, she had seen the coming of the railroad, the automobile, the telephone, electricity, indoor plumbing, the airplane, Sputnik, and credit cards. How amazing it must have been for her to think back to the "olden days," when drinking water was delivered by wagon in barrels, cloudy with a suspension of red clay that had to be filtered out before you could drink it. And to take a bath, you had to heat the water in a big cauldron on a wood-burning stove. We could scarcely believe that our elegant grandmother—the possessor of the famous string of black pearls she would show us if we were good—had grown up bathing in the kitchen and using an outhouse!

My grandmother's world may have been an endless round of tedious chores—yet, strangely, her stories paint a picture of an easygoing life with lots of time for family fun. By comparison, the world in which I raised my own children—hygienic and full of labor-saving conveniences though it was—seems stressful and hectic.

Living in the country, there was little entertainment to be had—unless you created it yourself. So several families would get together, pack covered wagons with supplies, and head off on a three-day fishing trip. Or they would ride out to a country church for "singing all day and supper on the ground." They picked wild plums and brought them home to make jelly and cobblers. They went to the fair held every year by the Civil War Veterans, where Pearl spent all her money on visits to the snake charmer. And they slept out on the porch on summer nights to watch the stars and tell ghost stories to the lonesome sound of a coyote's howl.

It seems to have been a perfect small-town childhood, ideal for encouraging independence, imagination, and self-confidence. And everything Pearl did was bathed in the warm glow of her father's love and attention. Dr. Bunkley must have had his faults, as we all do, but they were not apparent to Pearl. He comes across in her stories as a truly good man—resourceful, brave, honest, and cheerful. More to the point, he showed endless forbearance toward his willful and trouble-some daughter. In only one story do we see him lose his temper.

"My best friend had an older sister named Annie who was a great beauty and my ideal. Annie was a true 'lily of the field'—she toiled not. She sat around buffing her nails and massaging her elbows. It was fashionable in those days for ladies to 'swoon,' and Annie did so, very gracefully, on many occasions. One day, when my friend and I were playing, I decided to swoon. Mrs. Robertson was very upset. She washed my face with cold water, she chafed my wrists—but still I lay in my swoon. I was having a ball. She finally put me in the buggy and drove me home.

"They put me on Papa's big bed, but nothing would bring

me around, so they called for Papa to come home. If I had been smart, I would have 'come to' right then. But no. Papa walked over to the bed, lifted one eyelid, then gave me a big whack on the jaw. That brought me around in a hurry. It was the last of my swooning for life."

This event comes near the end of Pearl's long written narrative. By that time she was growing from a rambunctious youngster into a headstrong adolescent, and it would not be long before she and her beloved father would part. The final story, in fact, is a brief account of Papa's premature death—heroic to the last, prescribing for a patient from his sickbed, then refusing payment because the woman was a widow.

What is unusual and important about her description of her father's last hours is that she learned about them second-hand, presumably from her mother. Pearl had not been there at her father's bedside. She had not been there because he had refused to see her.

This part was left out of her written account—probably because it was too painful—but Pearl had told me about it one afternoon after I asked enough probing questions. As she explained why her father had turned away from his favorite child, I kept thinking how pointless and unnecessary it had all been.

Pearl had been engaged to a man, somewhat older than herself. He was well-off and respectable, and both her parents approved of the match. But Pearl did not love him.

Then she met my grandfather, Ernest Grissom. He was young, he was charming, and he sported a stylish pompadour.

Though the son of a farmer, Ernie had a college degree and good business sense. It's hard to imagine why Dr. Bunkley would find him objectionable. Perhaps it was just that Pearl had made a promise to her fiancé, and promises ought to be kept. Whatever the reason, Pearl and Ernie decided there was nothing for it but to elope.

To the best of my memory, the ceremony took place in a Model T Ford as they sped along—as fast as one *could* speed along on bad roads in a Model T Ford—toward the Oklahoma border. I am picturing a compliant judge in the back seat, as they jolted along over ruts and potholes, saying, "Do you"— bump, thump—"Pearl Bunkley, take this man. . . ?" with her papa barreling along after them. I can feel the hilarity, the excitement, the sheer *isn't-this-great?* wickedness of it all. She must not have realized how hard her father would take it.

Ernie proved to be a wonderful husband. He would be any father's dream son-in-law: He was successful and he was devoted to his wife. He made a small fortune in the department store trade and was elected mayor of Abilene, Texas. He used to go to New York on buying trips and come home with beautiful designer dresses and fine jewelry for Pearl. And he was fun to be with, sharing her creative spark and spirit of adventure. They were probably the happiest married couple I ever knew.

But my great-grandfather could not see into the future. He just knew his daughter had jilted one man and run off with another. Maybe, if he had lived a little longer, he would have gotten over it. But he died a month later. He never forgave her, and he never spoke to her again. Truly, Pearl's childhood was over.

Pearl now entered a time in her life that is mostly a blank to me. It was the time after her "little girl stories" stopped—now they were all about her children, like the time my mother shook the branches of a tree and said, "Look, Mother, this is what makes the wind blow"—and before my personal memories of her began. Only a few details survive, having been colorful enough to become part of our family lore.

I know that as a young bride, Pearl took up flying, one of the first women in Texas to do so. This was considered sufficiently exotic and newsworthy that she was asked to write a column about it for the *Abilene Reporter-News.* She called it "Sprouting Wings." I have a photograph of her in her flying gear: the leather helmet, goggles pushed up on her forehead, smart scarf around her neck.

Though I doubt Pearl had ever been out of Texas before that trip across the Oklahoma border, once she got a taste of travel she was hooked for life. This was not the kind of travel where you join a tour group and go from one European city to the next. This was the kind where you throw the kids in the back of the car and drive down to Mexico in the middle of a revolution.

Pearl had read somewhere that a place called Acapulco, in Mexico, had some of the most beautiful beaches in the world. So she decided to drive down there and see them. Her oldest child was no more than eleven, the youngest five or six, but this did not seem to worry her particularly. She loaded them into her snappy new Pierce Arrow and headed south. At one point the road became completely impassable. But this was a woman who had grown up in untamed country, forded rivers notorious for quicksand, and watched tornadoes from her upstairs porch. She was not about to turn around.

It was a time of civil war in Mexico and there were soldiers everywhere. Pearl approached a group of these *federales* and asked for help. For a certain sum of money, they agreed. So Pearl and her three children got out of the car and walked while the soldiers carried the car. Eventually they reached Acapulco. The beaches were indeed beautiful.

Wherever Pearl went—whether to Egypt or China or India or Guatemala—she would bring back art and textiles from these places and decorate her house with them. She had Mexican Santos, Greek icons, tiny embroidered Chinese shoes, and the side off a painted Sicilian cart. Needless to say, this kind of décor was not exactly the norm in West Texas in the fifties and sixties.

Looking back, it is clear that everything that is unique about my family began with Pearl. She set the standard we all tried to live up to.

She was the first of the "traveling Grissoms." The call of faraway places still whispers in our ears, three generations later. She was the first to collect art from all over the world, and she taught us to appreciate what beautiful objects could tell us about the culture and history of the people who made them. And she was the first to be published—first her newspaper articles and then a poem, written when she was eighty, that appeared in *The Lyric,* a small literary quarterly. Of her descendants, six of us—my mother, my cousin, my three children, and I—would go on to be published in books, magazines, or on the Internet. But Pearl was the pioneer.

In her final years, as the scope of her world was reduced to a cozy chair in her bedroom, Pearl began giving away her treasures. One Christmas I received an antique Imari bowl she had bought in Japan. Another year it was an Indian pot. And then, wonderfully, the black pearls. But best of all was the book of memories, the last outpouring of her fertile mind.

Of course, Pearl had been giving us treasures all her life. Here are a few she gave to me: a love of words and language, a fascination with faraway places and long-ago times, a sense of beauty, the joy of making things with my hands. She taught me that it is all right to be different, and that if you don't take risks, you'll never have an adventure.

After her funeral, the family gathered at her house and started telling "Pearl stories." We stayed there till dark, talking and remembering and laughing. The stories and the semi-hysterical laughter they generated were a tremendous release, an act of love and gratitude for the woman whose spirit had showed us how to set out, each on our own individual path, armed only—*only!*—with imagination, an independent spirit, and a love of learning. The sad, confused woman had disappeared and the old Pearl was back. She will always be with me.

When I was asked to participate in this project, I was delighted. It would give me a chance to honor my grandmother, Pearl, who was both my spiritual mentor and a really interesting person. What's more, I had in my hands a 67-page manuscript of my grandmother's memories, written in her own words, describing events dating back to 1896. With such a rich resource, both revealing of her personality and fascinating to read, I thought I should just step back and let Pearl tell her own story. And in the first draft, that is exactly what I did. Then six months passed, and I went on to other projects. When the manuscript came back to be edited, I faced the challenge of cutting it almost in half and—more importantly—bringing myself more into the story. What was my relationship with Pearl? Why was she so important to me?

As I worked on the story, I found myself digging deeper into exactly what it was about my grandmother that made her so memorable, why I so loved spending time with her, and how she marked my life and that of her entire family. My grandmother's "little girl stories" took on added resonance, and I truly saw the young Pearl for the first time—a troublesome, hard-headed free spirit, growing up in a flat and dusty small town protected and adored by her wise and loving Papa, Atticus Finch with a doctor's bag.

My mother used to say that "good writing is clear thinking." I think that is true. You have to keep writing and rewriting until you truly understand your subject and what it is you are trying to say. Writing this story about my grandmother began in my head and ended in my heart. It brought me closer to her than I have been since she died, more than twenty years ago. And it was a precious journey.

Grandma and Her Needle

G oody-goody gumdrop!" I sang whenever Mother told me we were going to visit my grandparents. This meant a train journey, all of twenty miles. In 1920, when I was an only child living on a farm outside of Yamhill, Oregon, pop. 366, the trip to Banks, pop. 209, was an adventure, something to hop up and down and sing about.

First, Mother and I walked the mile through Yamhill to the yellow depot. I loved the excitement of seeing the locomotive chugging down the track trailing a plume of smoke. We climbed onto the train and settled ourselves on the scratchy green upholstery. "Board!" the conductor shouted, and we were off! I waved to little boys sitting on fence posts watching the train go by. How superior I felt, riding in style, leaving them behind. Poor little boys.

At Banks we detrained at another yellow depot exactly like the first and walked to the two-storied building with W. S. ATLEE GENERAL MERCHANDISE painted across the false front. My grandparents hurried to the door to meet us, Grandpa in his flannel shirt and baggy pants held up by suspenders—"galluses," he called them—and Grandma wearing a neat cotton dress and a white apron. Grandpa was small and spry. Grandma was short and regretted her "tendency to put on flesh."

My grandparents lived upstairs over the store, not that they spent much time there. The store was a busy place, the center of Banks. Early in the morning, customers banged on the door calling, "Open up! Open up!" while Grandpa, pulling on his pants, shouted, "Hold your horses! I'm coming! I'm coming!"

By midmorning, old men were gathered around the wood stove to talk politics while they waited for the morning paper to arrive at the post office next door. All day, Grandpa served the people of Banks, grinding coffee beans, cutting cheese, filling cans with "coal oil" for kerosene lamps, climbing a ladder to reach canned goods on high shelves, snapping open paper bags and filling them with rice or tea. Overalls, work shoes, and straw hats stocked the shelves at the rear of the store. Saturday night, bearded loggers clomped through the doors to buy work clothes or supplies of beans and coffee for the week. Evenings people came to sit around the stove and visit with their neighbors.

All this interested me, but it was Grandma's side of the store that I loved most of all. There was so much to look at: the case of colorful spools of thread and embroidery cotton, laces, hair nets, corsets, stockings, bolts of flannel, flowered percale, muslin, and two bolts of woolen serge—one navy blue and one brown—which I thought ugly, but Mother said were beautiful quality.

After Grandma had washed the breakfast dishes, swept the floor, and made the bed, she descended the wooden stairs to preside over the dry goods in her gentle, quiet way, helping women match thread to fabric, unfurling bolts of percale, measuring and cutting while she listened to her customers talk about the price of sugar, the number of jars of fruit they had canned, the pillowcases they were embroidering, and in lowered voices with a glance at me, the scandalous behavior of some of their neighbors.

Grandma had another talent. Hats! In the corner room at the head of the stairs was her millinery shop, a fascinating place to explore. Grandpa had built tables and shelves for untrimmed hats, both straw and felt, boxes of artificial flowers and cherries, real feathers and silky ostrich plumes, bolts of veiling, and spools of ribbon, all waiting for Grandma's artistic eye and skillful fingers. Grandma never minded my rummaging through boxes or trying on hats in front of the mirror, turning this way and that, admiring myself, pretending I was a grown-up customer.

One afternoon, when I was about five years old, a farm wagon driven by a woman accompanied by five little girls, stair steps in size, pulled up in front of the store. They were Belgian refugees from World War I who had settled near Banks. The mother explained in broken English that because they were Catholic her daughters had to have hats to wear to church. All she could afford were cheap straw hats, the sort of hats farmers wore in the fields.

Five disappointed faces touched Grandma's heart. Of course, little girls wanted pretty hats. "Come with me," she said, and led the way upstairs to her millinery shop, where she found shopworn flowers and faded ribbons no one wanted to buy. Grandma's nimble fingers and practiced eye quickly turned those field hats into creations that made five little girls happy. They thanked her and went hopping down the stairs and through the store. Grandma smiled as she watched them ride off in the big wagon with their ribbons and flowers fluttering in the breeze.

As much as I enjoyed Grandma's millinery shop, there was one hat I did not like one bit—my Sunday school hat. When Grandma took the train to the wholesale house in Portland to buy merchandise, she brought back for me a black Italian straw hat, which she trimmed with a black grosgrain ribbon band and streamers that hung down past my shoulder blades. I hated the hot, heavy hat. When it blew off, Mother secured it with a white elastic band under my chin. I scowled and chewed the elastic whenever I was forced to wear it. "Beverly, stop that!" said my exasperated mother.

In spite of the soggy elastic, women stopped on the street to say, "What a beautiful hat!" I sulked beneath the broad brim.

"Beverly, behave yourself," said Mother. "It's a lovely hat. Other little girls would be happy to have a hat like yours." I knew better than to answer, but I secretly thought, I bet they wouldn't.

One breezy day, the ribbons blew over my shoulder and flapped into the ice-cream cone I was eating. Goody, I thought. Now maybe Mother would throw away that hat and

I would be free. But no. Grandma retrimmed it with fresh ribbon, and while she was at it redyed it with smelly liquid from a bottle. "It looks like new," said Mother. I was afraid she was right.

"Beverly, get that look off your face," ordered Daddy when once again I was forced to wear that hat. My stinky hat, I thought but did not say. I don't know what finally happened to my Italian straw hat, but it seemed to me that I wore it for years. In those frugal days, when I finally outgrew it, Mother probably passed it on to another unfortunate little girl to sulk under.

Grandma also made my dresses, printed dresses with matching bloomers, sailor dresses with white braid trimming the collars, scratchy organdy party dresses, and one accordion-pleated red dress for very special occasions. When she noticed my interest in sewing, she gave me a large darning needle I could thread myself and four squares of printed fabric, two pink and two blue. She showed me how to piece them together to make a doll's quilt. I sat on the floor and struggled to sew with small stitches. When I finished, I was so pleased with what I had done that I added a piece of lace across the square to make it prettier. Mother proudly pasted my quilt into my book of baby pictures.

After that, whenever we visited the store, my first question was "Are there any remnants for doll clothes?" Grandma always smiled and answered, "I think we can find some," and cut a few inches from new fabrics for me. I worked hard on those doll clothes, trimming them with tucks and ruffles.

As the years went by, my father decided he had had enough of farming. We moved to Portland, away from the fields and orchards, the barn and windmill, the cows and pigs and chickens, but we still returned to Banks by train, then by bus ("stage," Grandpa called it), and finally by one of the first Model A Chevrolets, which my father bought and taught himself to drive by reading a book of directions.

By the seventh grade, I had advanced to sewing for myself because Mother's careless sewing did not measure up to Grandma's. I began with bloomers and nightgowns and then, with the help of school sewing classes, dresses. When we visited Banks, Grandma praised my work, but Grandpa was too worried to notice. A chain store had opened in Forest Grove, less than ten miles away, competition for the proprietor of a small general merchandise store to worry about.

Then, in the late 1920s, the Depression hit. Grandpa frowned as he figured on the backs of envelopes. When I asked what he was figuring, he answered, "Profit and loss." Before long, people could no longer afford to build houses. Logging declined because no one bought lumber. No loggers stomped into the store on Saturday night.

More and more shamefaced customers asked if their purchases could be "put on the books." Kindhearted Grandpa was generous with credit. "I can't bear to see little young-uns go without," he said. Women buying fabric brought their patterns to Grandma, who spread her percale or muslin on the counter and carefully laid out pattern pieces to show how her customers could save every inch of fabric.

"Dad-burned chain store," grumped Grandpa. The people of Banks had begun to go to Forest Grove to pay cash for lower prices. The chain store did not offer credit. Grandpa's supplies of groceries dwindled, but he still let poor people charge. Even though newspapers no longer arrived by mail, old men continued to gather around the big black stove to "chew the fat" over politics. They hoped "this feller Roosevelt could pull the country out of its slump."

Women could no longer afford to buy new hats or even to have their old hats retrimmed. The flowers and ribbons in the millinery shop grew dusty. Grandma looked sad. I'm sure she missed the one bit of extravagance in Banks. Shelves of dry goods now had little left to offer, only the bolts of navy blue and brown serge remained untouched.

By the 1930s, I was busy with high school studies and activities and usually stayed home when Mother went to visit my grandparents. When I was about to go away to college in Southern California, Mother brought home two dress lengths of that serviceable navy blue and brown serge. "Oh, Mother," I protested in dismay when she gave them to me. "They're so *ugly*."

Mother sighed. "Times are hard," she reminded me. "Every nickel has to do the work of two."

Mother didn't need to tell me about hard times. Everyone I knew was feeling the pinch. Reluctantly, I made two dresses, lightening the blue with a red-and-white ruffled collar and the brown with embroidery. "Beautiful work," the neighbors said, but I don't recall wearing those dresses more than once or twice in California, where the climate was warmer and girls dressed more casually. Besides, the dresses made me itch.

When I was a senior in college, Grandpa unexpectedly died and Grandma, now failing, came to live with my parents. The store building was sold to a couple who wanted it because the store had meant so much to them when they were young and poor and had no place else to go in the evening. They tore off the upstairs rooms and turned the store into living quarters. I remember wondering what had happened to the rest of the navy blue and brown serge Mother had left behind when she moved Grandma from Banks to Portland.

Grandma, always a quiet woman, grew even more quiet as her mind seemed to drift away. She called me Mable, my mother's name, and referred to my father as "that gentleman." Mother placed her in a chair by the front window so she could watch neighbors come and go. "But she has nothing to do," said Mother, and finally, in desperation, she cut holes in our dish towels for Grandma to mend. She sat sewing with tiny, perfect stitches, as neat as those I had tried to copy when I was a little girl. She looked serene and content as she sat stitching on those dish towels by the front window.

Grandma died a few years after I was married and busy making curtains and a braided rug for my own home. Like Grandma, I was stitching my way through life, making my own clothes, our children's clothes, and once, during World War II, when there was almost no merchandise in stores, I made a pair of shorts for my husband from a printed luncheon cloth I did not like. "I feel as if I am wearing a sarong," he said as he gamely wore those shorts. Later, after our children were grown, I designed and made needlepoint tapestries depicting our family, our house, and the apple tree in the backyard. Now I am planning another for our grandchildren.

Thank you, Grandma, for giving me a love of sewing.

GAIL CARSON LEVINE

A Visit to Grandma's

The visit takes place on a fall day in 1961. I was four-teen, and I was walking to Grandma's apartment with Mommy and Daddy, which is what I called my parents till they died when I was in my late thirties. Grandma lived with my mother's unmarried sisters, Aunt Harriet and Aunt Fossie, whose real name was Roslyn. My grandfather had died three years earlier.

At Grandma's we were expecting to visit for a half hour or so before the whole family went to a neighborhood Chinese restaurant for four dinners from Column A and two from Column B.

On the way over, Mommy and Daddy weren't talking to me. They were mad because my room was a mess, and because I almost never helped around the house. I'd protested that I was studying nonstop. This wasn't completely true, but I was having a hard tenth grade. I'd added that my room was mine and they didn't have to look at it if they didn't want to.

That's when they stopped talking to me. I didn't talk to them either, but inside I was close to surrender. I could never hold on to a position for long when they froze me out.

At Grandma's, Aunt Harriet let us in. I entered behind my parents and hung back, wishing I could be invisible and avoid kissing anybody. As usual, I smelled Grandma's cooking. Her house always smelled this way, dense and a little scorched. As far as I knew, Grandma only cooked stew and pot roast. No matter how often we visited, she served one or the other.

"We're not going out to eat," Aunt Harriet said.

"Oh?" Mommy said. "Why not?"

Grandma came out of the kitchen. "Where's Gail?"

"Here," I said, because I had to.

Aunt Fossie came out of the bedroom she and Aunt Harriet shared. The six of us were crowded into Grandma's narrow hallway.

"Give me your coats," Aunt Fossie said.

"Give your grandma a kiss."

I edged around Mommy to get to her. When I reached her, Grandma's smell overpowered the cooking smell. I knew she was clean, but she didn't smell of soap or shampoo or anything pleasant. She had a sour body odor. I held my breath and kissed her cheek. Her skin felt soft and loose.

She held me close for a few seconds, and a plastic button on her housedress dug into my chest. Then she kissed my temple and let me go. I backed up a step and breathed again. I was sure she'd left lipstick lips on my face.

"We're not eating out," Aunt Harriet announced, "because we can't afford to."

"Is this how you let her leave the house?" Grandma said to

Mommy. "No hat? She'll get sick, Tsippe."

Tsippe was my mother's Jewish name, which she hated. Her regular name was Sylvia.

"It's not that cold," I said, defending Mommy and me. "It's only October." I wanted to say, *How do you know how cold it is? Have you been outside? How come you always know what's best for everybody?*

But I never told Grandma or the aunts what I was thinking.

I took off my coat and gave it and my handbag to Aunt Fossie.

She said, "I'm putting everything on the bed in Mama's room."

I'd started disliking Grandma and Aunt Fossie and Aunt Harriet years and years ago, the first time I heard them criticize Mommy.

I was probably five or six. I had spent the night at Grandma's, although I don't remember why. After breakfast I stayed in the dining room to color in a coloring book that Mommy had brought from home. Grandma and Aunt Harriet and Aunt Fossie were in the kitchen, and I could hear everything they said.

"Do you know what Tsippe gives her for breakfast every day?" Grandma said.

"No, what?" Aunt Fossie asked.

"Nothing would surprise me," Aunt Harriet said.

I colored outside the line, which annoyed me.

"Gail says she always has six slices of Wonder bread

with the crusts taken off."

"That's all?" Aunt Fossie said, sounding shocked. "Not even any juice?"

"No juice, and Tsippe can't even be bothered to toast the bread or shmear anything on it."

I did have juice, but I had forgotten to mention it, and Mommy wanted to toast the bread, but I wouldn't eat it if she did. Untoasted Wonder bread was like edible Play-Doh. I could squeeze the bread and shape it, and then I could eat it. Or I could squeeze it in my mouth. I loved it.

"At least I got a decent breakfast into her today."

I realized then that I shouldn't have told what I usually had for breakfast and I should have turned down the French toast and oatmeal Grandma had served me. The French toast had been okay, but I'd eaten the oatmeal only because I was allowed to add as much brown sugar as I wanted.

After that visit, I never relaxed again when Grandma or the aunts were around. I acted like a teenager when I was with them long before I became one. My face froze into a solemn mask, and I gave one-word answers when they spoke to me.

Maybe I would have forgiven them if Mommy could have shrugged off their criticism. But she couldn't, and she was often miserable. They didn't find fault only with my upbringing. They criticized Mommy for not visiting them often enough. If she bought a coat, they suggested she shouldn't have spent money on herself. If she and Daddy bought furniture, the aunts and Grandma didn't like the color or said we hadn't gotten a good buy.

Not that they ever came out and said what they meant. They wouldn't say, *Tsippe, you are a rotten mother.* Or, *Tsippe, you are a selfish spendthrift.*

Instead, one of them might say, *I wish I could buy myself a coat like that.* Or, *Tsippe, I saw a good sale on couches in the paper.*

So on this particular day I went to Mommy and whispered, "I'll clean up my room, and I'll help out more."

But I should have said it on the walk over. It would have meant something then. Mommy nodded, but I could tell she wasn't thinking about me anymore.

"Why can't we afford to go out?" she asked.

Grandma ignored the question and said, "What did Gail whisper to you, Tsippe? Gail, what did you tell Mommy?"

"Nothing," I said.

Mommy said, "She promised to clean up her room and help more at home."

"She's just a baby," Grandma said, "and she studies so much. When she grows up she'll keep her room clean."

I hated having Grandma stand up for me—because she was criticizing Mommy again. I found myself saying, "I don't study *that* much."

Daddy shrugged out of his coat, and Aunt Fossie took it. Even with my coat off I was sweating. Grandma's apartment was always overheated.

"Come inside," Grandma said. "Sit awhile."

We all trooped into the living room, which had the piano nobody played and the glass candy dishes filled with candy no one ever ate, except me sometimes. The couches and chairs were covered with plastic slipcovers to protect the upholstery. I always wondered who Grandma took the plastic off for. She never had for us, no matter what the occasion was.

I sat on the couch next to Mommy. Daddy was on the other side of her. The plastic crickled and crackled when we sat. Plastic slipcovers had to be the hottest material in the world. I felt sweat trickle down from my armpit.

I was in the middle of reading *Hawaii*, and the book was in my bag in Grandma's room. I was itching to get it and read, but I knew Mommy and Daddy would think I was being rude.

Aunt Fossie sat on the far end of the couch, then stood again. I liked her better than Aunt Harriet. "Can I get anybody some icebox water?"

We all said yes, and Aunt Fossie started to leave the room.

Aunt Harriet said, "We can't eat out because Mama lost a hundred dollars yesterday."

Daddy whistled. Nobody said anything. Aunt Fossie stopped between Grandma's chair and the door.

I wondered how Grandma could have lost so much money. In 1961, a hundred dollars was two months' rent. I thought maybe I could find the money. Searching for it would give me something to do, which would be much better than sitting here.

"Where did you see it last?" I said. "When did you lose it?" I slid my hand behind me, between the cushion and the back of the couch. The money could be buried in the upholstery and not be found for years.

Nobody answered me. Aunt Harriet said something to Mommy in Yiddish.

Grandma said, "I'll put up water for the noodles." She left the living room.

"It's a sickness," Aunt Fossie said. "You can't blame her."

"Who's to blame then?" Aunt Harriet said. "Rozzy, did you lose a hundred dollars in a poker game? Tsippe, did you?"

Grandma lost the money gambling!

I'd known about her card playing for as long as I could remember. Every week she went to somebody's house to play, and she and the other people paid the hostess for having the game, and the hostess served food to the players. I knew this because Grandma would make snide remarks about the food that was served or the cleanliness of the hostess's apartment.

I also knew that Grandma usually lost. But I'd always imagined a bunch of old ladies playing for pennies. It had never crossed my mind that she could lose more than a few dollars.

I felt a little sorry for her, for doing something so crazy and getting everybody mad at her.

Aunt Fossie sat on the couch again. "We'll have to get our deposits back for those dresses, Harriet. Tsippe, you should have seen them. Silk. Twenty percent off at Ohrbach's."

Aunt Harriet shook her head. "I'm still getting my dress. The dress is a drop in the bucket."

"She hasn't lost so much in years," Mommy said.

Aunt Harriet snapped, "What do you care? It isn't your problem."

Mommy looked down and began to pick at a psoriasis scab on her elbow. I wanted to punch Aunt Harriet.

Aunt Fossie said, "They have a family to support."

Daddy's face was bright red. He stood and took out his wallet and handed some money to Aunt Harriet. I couldn't see how much.

"I would have given you this anyway. You didn't have to make a crack."

Aunt Fossie said, "Harriet didn't mean—"

Aunt Harriet said, "I just hope I can get my money back for Florida. I can't go now."

She'd been planning to go there on her Christmas vacation.

"You should still go," Aunt Fossie said. "I can cancel my trip. I don't mind. I can go to Washington another time."

"You're right," Aunt Harriet said. "Washington isn't far."

Aunt Harriet was amazing. She always got what she wanted, one way or another.

Grandma yelled from the kitchen that dinner was ready, and we all filed into the dining room. During the meal no one said anything about the hundred dollars, but Grandma talked about her gambling.

"I like to gamble," she said. "It's my only pleasure. I don't buy myself silk dresses. I don't go on fancy vacations. I don't begrudge anyone else their pleasures."

I wondered if she was going to her game this week.

Nobody said anything for a few minutes. Then Daddy asked Grandma what was going on in the soap operas she loved to watch. She launched into a detailed update of the saga of each of her "shows."

I wished dinner was ice cream, not hot chicken soup followed by hot pot roast and noodles and canned string beans. I ate because I was hungry, and I got hotter. I could have been served as the next course, roasted granddaughter.

I wished I could be somewhere cooler. I wished I could be somewhere *else*.

Grandma finished talking about her soap operas. Mommy and the aunts began complaining about their schools and their principals. They all taught in elementary schools in New York City. I started worrying about my French test on Monday. In my mind I conjugated *avoir* and *être*. Grandma dished out applesauce for dessert. There was a seed in my portion, which I accidentally bit down on. It tasted bitter.

After dinner we went back to the living room, and Grandma turned on the TV. I went to the bathroom. Afterward, I stood in the living room doorway. Nobody turned my way. They were all engrossed in *The Jackie Gleason Show*.

I tiptoed down the hall. It would be great to stand outside the apartment for a few minutes and cool off. I turned the lower lock. It didn't make a sound. Then I opened the upper lock. It turned noisily.

Daddy called, "What are you doing?"

"I'm just going to stand in the hallway for a few minutes. I'll be right back."

Nobody told me not to. I stepped out and closed the door behind me. It was at least twenty degrees cooler out here.

I wondered who lived behind the other doors. In our building we knew almost everyone. The people across from

Grandma had already put their garbage out for the super to pick up: three brown paper bags with grease stains.

A door down the hall opened. An elderly man came out. He locked his door and rang for the elevator. In a minute or two, it came.

The man held the elevator door open. "You going down, girlie?"

I was too embarrassed to explain that I was just standing in the hall. Besides, I wanted to go out.

"Thanks!" I ran into the elevator.

It was much colder outside, and there was a sharp wind. It felt great.

I walked along the wall of the J. Hood Wright Park. I wondered if anyone had come out of Grandma's looking for me yet. Daddy might have. He probably wanted to get away as much as I did. On the other hand, he loved Jackie Gleason.

Why did we have to go to Grandma's week after week? I knew Mommy and Daddy didn't enjoy themselves either. Why did they have to be so dutiful?

Earlier that fall, I used to sit on the park wall in the evenings and hang out with my friends. That was before it got dark so early and before we started having so many tests.

I realized that it might not be safe here. Anybody could be in the park at night and could jump out at me. The neighborhood was quiet now, and the closest person was a block away. I crossed the street and headed toward Broadway, hugging myself for warmth. The heat at Grandma's was beginning to seem inviting, but I wasn't ready to go back yet.

Why didn't Mommy ever stick up for herself? Why couldn't she say something to Grandma and Aunt Harriet?

Well, she grew up there, so she might not know how to say anything—she might be too used to knuckling under. But why didn't Daddy say anything?

I turned the corner onto Broadway. The drugstore was still open, and so was the Good Luck Chinese restaurant, but everything else was closed.

If Mommy and Daddy wouldn't say anything, that left me. I was the right one to tell off Grandma and the aunts, even though Mommy and Daddy wouldn't want me to. They'd think I was "starting up," making trouble. But they'd be glad in the end, if it cleared the air and if the aunts and Grandma stopped hurting Mommy.

Maybe I wouldn't even have to be rude. I could just be calm and polite and reasonable.

I stopped walking. How could I say how spiteful and underhanded they were without sounding rude?

Well, I could start by telling them that I was sure they wanted us to have a decent time—no, a nice time—when we came over. But we couldn't because of the way they acted. I'd assure them that I knew they didn't intend to make anyone feel bad. Then I'd give a few factual examples of things they'd said. I wouldn't change anything. It would be their words, so they'd have to admit they'd been mean and nasty.

I looked at my watch in the light of a street lamp. *The Jackie Gleason Show* would be over in seven minutes, and someone would definitely come out after me then. I hurried back, hoping nobody would look too closely at me when I got inside or they'd see how red my cheeks were from the cold.

While I waited for the elevator, I started getting nervous about what I was going to say. When the elevator came, a lady and her daughter, who was about seven, were inside, riding up from the basement. They got off on the second floor.

My heart started to pound. The elevator stopped at three, but nobody got on. I pressed six again. I wanted to get there and get it over with.

The elevator stopped at four, and I realized that the lady's daughter had pressed all the floors. I was going to be berserk by the time I got to six.

I got to six. Two minutes left in *The Jackie Gleason Show*. I was freezing, but my palms were sweating. I opened the door to Grandma's.

They hadn't noticed how long I'd been gone. I sat on the couch between Mommy and Daddy.

The show ended, and a commercial came on. My heart was still pounding. Maybe this was the wrong time to speak up. Maybe I should wait for Grandma or one of the aunts to say the next thing to make Mommy feel bad. It wouldn't seem out of the blue then, and I knew I wouldn't have to wait long.

A variety special came on. A woman in a sequined gown sang "Misty."

"Look at her," Grandma said. "She's not wearing anything under that gown. It's a schande!" *Schande* meant disgrace.

I couldn't believe it. "You don't even know her," I blurted out. "And you're criticizing her."

Everybody looked at me. It seemed like the TV volume went way down.

"Criticize? What criticize?" Grandma said. "They're all like that, entertainers."

"It's not just entertainers. You do it all the time."

"Gail . . . ," Mommy said warningly.

Daddy put his hand on my shoulder.

But I'd gone too far to stop. "Before, you blamed Mommy because you didn't think I'd dressed warmly enough, and Aunt Harriet blamed her for not caring about you losing your money."

Aunt Harriet stood up. "How dare you—"

"Shah, Harriet," Grandma said. "It's just a phase. She's a teenager. The baby's a teenager now."

I wanted to scream, *It's not a phase!* but Daddy said, "Enough, Gail." His face was bright red again.

I almost said, *It's not enough*, but Mommy was sitting extra straight and picking at the scab again.

"Oh, forget it." I stood up and went into Grandma's bedroom. I was angry at everyone, Mommy and Daddy included. Couldn't they tell I was trying to help them? Why weren't they proud of me? I fought back tears.

They were all probably discussing me. I left Grandma's room and tiptoed back toward the living room. I stopped in the hall and listened.

". . . say such things," Aunt Harriet was saying. "You didn't teach her any respect, Tsippe."

"If you had talked that way to me," Grandma said, "I would have washed your mouth out good with soap."

They were blaming Mommy.

Daddy said, "She didn't mean anything."

Aunt Fossie said, "Things have changed since we grew up."

"So you think it's all right, Rozzy?" Aunt Harriet said.

I peeked in. Mommy was still picking at her scab.

I went back to Grandma's room. I was crying. I threw myself on the bed and buried my head in Daddy's coat. I should have kept my mouth shut. I should have known that Grandma and the aunts would have an answer for anything I said. I had made everything worse.

But I had tried to make everything better.

Mommy and Daddy didn't understand. They probably wouldn't be talking to me worse than before. I struggled to catch my breath from crying.

I opened Grandma's window and stuck my head out, crying down on Ft. Washington Avenue.

Finally the tears stopped. I brought my head back in and closed the window. I found my bag and dried my eyes with tissues. Then I took out *Hawaii* and sat on the bed and read till it was time to go home.

AUTHOR'S NOTE

My father was an orphan, and so I had only one grandmother, my mother's mother. I've been told that she had a terrific sense of humor. I've been told that her home was always open to her children's friends. I've been told that she was strong willed, enough to make sure that her daughters completed college, even during the Depression and even though the family was very poor.

But I didn't experience Grandma's best qualities.

This story is cobbled together out of real events and a few inventions. The real people who are the characters behave as I think they would have, except me. I was never quite as brave as the Gail in the story.

And Then Another Locust Came and Took Away Another Grain of Corn

As I made my bed this morning, I thought of my Grandmother Johnson. It was she who taught me to get up, turn around, and make it then and there. "A bed made at once," she would say as she flapped air through the sheets, "saves time in the crunch."

Grandmother Johnson, my mother's mother, was a finely balanced mix of humor and realism. "Do it now" was her approach, not only to bed making but to all tasks. With this axiom she moved through her day, accomplishing wonders. She made stunning dresses and hats for her four daughters, baked delectable pies and breads, cooked unforgettable meals, cleaned, washed and ironed, carried dinners to sick relatives. And, because she did these tasks as they presented themselves, she also had time to read.

"Read," she would say to her grandchildren. "Reading is the sunshine and rain of the mind."

I find no mention in family memoirs about Grandmother's schooling. I think she went no further than the seventh grade. After that, she spent a great deal of her free time in the library reading herself into the equivalent of a high school education.

Grandmother's full name was Mary Agnes Aitcheson Johnson. Agnes was born in Maryland of a first-generation Scotch family who steered themselves through life with old-world wisdom, such as "Never spend all you make."

Grandmother Johnson repeated these wisdoms to us in great fun as well as in seriousness. We laughed at their con-tradictions. There are counter-gems for each gem of advice: "Absence makes the heart grow fonder" was canceled by "Out of sight, out of mind." My twin brothers, Frank and John, chortled over "Beauty is skin deep, ugliness goes to the bone."

When my cousins, Ellen and Paula, and I were old enough to appreciate the adages, we asked Grandmother to write them down. She was eighty-three at the time and her eyesight was failing, but each morning after breakfast she wrote in twelve little black books for her twelve grandchildren 100 maxims to live by. She entitled each book, "Things to Remember." Today I recall her saying as she gave me my book, "Always remember, 'It's not what you do, it's what you are.'"

Grandmother was born in 1857 in Laurel, Maryland, fif-teen years after her parents and grandparents emigrated from Paisley, Scotland, in the tall ship *Columbia*. They eventually settled in Ellerslie, or "Scotchtown," near Laurel. When Grandmother was twelve years old, she moved with her par-ents to Alexandria, Virginia. She lived the remaining eighty-four of her ninety-six years in that historic and interesting town.

She grew to be a beautiful young woman. I have a picture of her in her twenties. Her long hair is braided in a ring around the back of her head, sunny auburn curls fall softly against her cheeks. Her large eyes, a deep blue, make her transparent skin fairly glow. The bones of her face are delicate. Said her sister, Mag, of Grandmother to her daughters: "None of you will ever be as beautiful as your mother."

Grandmother loved good stories. She not only told them but was the protagonist of many. Her courtship is one. On a rainy day, Agnes, then sixteen, came out of the town drugstore into a downpour. Suddenly an umbrella sheltered her. Holding it was handsome John Weidon Johnson, a young man she had never met but knew well of. He had given a high school graduation speech entitled "Woman's Influence." "And there," Grandmother recalled, "umbrella over me, stood the man who had discussed the importance of a mother's influence on her children. He requested to see me home in the rain."

John, or Jack as he was called, did not take the direct route home. Instead, to Grandmother's delight, he took the most circuitous route he could find. But after that lovely day Jack did not speak to her when they met on the street. He would only make a courteous bow with a sweep of his hat and pass by. "How hurtful," I said when I first heard this story, but I did not know how socially correct my grandfather had been. Jack was playing the role of a proper nineteenth-century gentleman.

Many months later, he inveigled the lovely Agnes's

brothers to invite him to their house. In the living room of the Aitcheson home, on Christmas Day, Agnes and Jack were "formally introduced."

After that Jack could "come calling," and call he did. Having often noticed Agnes reading in the library, he arrived almost every day with books from his father's own library. Eagerly my book-loving grandmother became a fan of Sir Walter Scott, Charles Dickens, Henry Wadsworth Longfellow, and other nineteenth-century writers.

Their courtship continued until Jack felt he could support a wife—six years. They were finally married in 1879.

After their fourth child was born, they built a home at 509 Duke Street in Alexandria. It still stands, a brown-brick town house with a small backyard enclosed by a tall wooden fence. In short order, its banisters were polished by the seats of their sons Albert's and John's pants and the living room was turned over to sewing and reading. On Sunday evenings "the Uncles," Grandmother's four bachelor brothers, played violin concerts or wound up the mahogany Victrola and listened to Enrico Caruso on RCA Victor Gold Seal records.

Of all the stories about Grandmother, my favorite is what I call "Aunt Polly and the Rain." With its first telling I became aware of Grandmother's love and reasonableness. It goes like this: Grandmother spanked Aunt Polly for something she did not do. When Polly wailed in protest, Grandmother promised that the next time she was due a spanking to remind her and she would not get one.

A season passed, then one rainy day four bored girls were running out of the house into the rain, screaming and giggling.

Grandmother asked them to stop. They persisted. "The next one who runs out in the rain," Grandmother snapped, "gets a spanking." That was warning enough. The girls stayed inside, except, to her sisters' gaping horror, Aunt Polly. She sashayed out into the rain and opened her mouth to catch the drops while flicking her petticoats.

"Mother," one of the girls cried out. "Pauline disobeyed. She's out in the rain."

Grandmother took Polly into the pantry for the spanking. The three sisters listened and waited. No wails or cries were heard. Presently Aunt Polly walked out, head up and smiling.

"Why didn't Mother spank you?" Aunt Catherine asked. "You were bad."

"I reminded her that she had already given me my spanking," Polly said, and sauntered off.

These splendid days came to a sudden end. Grandfather Johnson died of a heart attack at age fifty-one. There were no pensions, no social securities, no life insurance plans to fill in for the death of a breadwinner.

These were dark days for the family. My mother and Aunt Polly gave up their dreams of going to college and went to work at the Smithsonian Institution in Washington, D.C., as entomology assistants. Aunt Catherine taught school and went to night school, and Uncle John worked and studied law. Uncle Albert, the oldest son, could not help very much. He now had a family in Madison, Wisconsin.

To make ends meet, Grandmother Johnson made dresses for her working daughters, pressed their clothes, and fixed meals. Her cousin, Judith, who lived on a farm in Virginia, sent her hams, flour, vegetables, fowl, and her famous pastries.

I always imagined Grandmother facing her grief and deprivations with these words that she wrote in my book, "The best laid plans o' mice and men gang aft a gleey," then turning around and making the bed.

I did not realize that I had a loving relationship with Grandmother until I was six or seven. She was simply the grand lady at the head of the Thanksgiving and Christmas dinner table, dressed in softly colored blouses trimmed with handmade lace, who tolerated giggling girls and noisy boys.

But between holidays, when she would visit our home in Washington, D.C., I came to see her love for me. My brothers were merciless teasers and could reduce me to tears with a couple of words or a joke. She saw and understood my pain. However, rather than reprimand them, which wouldn't have done any good, she took me aside.

"The next time they tease you," she said, "smile. That's the worst thing you can do to them." This was painful advice, and I chose to ignore it until the day John and Frank fed me "a delicious bite" of an elephant ear leaf. If ever there was a moment to try out Grandmother Johnson's antidote for teasers, this was it. Elephant ear stings the tongue like needles and pins and I knew it, but I took the bite. With my mouth burning, my ears ringing, I looked from one twin to the other and—smiled. That was the last practical joke they pulled on me. But to this day I wished I had kicked them.

Grandmother could also cure giggling girls. My cousins, Ellen and Paula, and I were regularly sent from Christmas or

Thanksgiving tables for getting the giggles.

One memorable dinner, in a moment of silence, Great-Uncle Johnny Aitcheson burped long and loudly. I can still feel the pain of trying to stifle my laughter. My throat burned. My ears rang. I looked at Ellen. Fatally, our eyes met and we broke into uncontrollable giggles. Paula joined in. Our parents tried to shame us into silence. The uncles and aunts told us we were spoiling their dinner, which only set us off in wilder giggles.

Then Grandmother spoke up. "Let them giggle," she said. And that did it. There was not a laugh left in us. The spasm was over. We had been freed from ourselves.

"You don't stop the breach in the dike with fire," Grandmother said, and the family was satisfied with whatever that meant. To this day I think she made it up on the spur of the moment. It is not in my little black book.

When I visited Grandmother, I would beg her to tell me stories "about what she did when she was a little girl." I could not hear too often how she got her hand stuck in the cookie jar, like the proverbial monkey, when her mother caught her stealing sweets. I wanted to hear again and again how my great-grandmother Johnson took medicine and supplies to both Confederate and Union soldiers in prisons in Alexandria. Alexandria was an occupied city at the time, and Great-Grandmother had to get passes to visit relatives south of the city. When she did, she carried medicines and supplies in her petticoats through the Yankee lines to the Confederate soldiers. She smuggled more than supplies. When Confederate

General J. E. B. Stuart lost the plume he always wore in his hat, somehow Great-Grandmother managed to carry a new one to him.

Other than the telling of these stories, Grandmother never discussed the Civil War. I eventually understood why. "Brothers fought and killed brothers," she said one day when the subject came up, and her eyes filmed over with pain.

I particularly loved Grandmother Johnson to tell me stories of the ingenuity and fearlessness of the women in the family. The one about "Awesome Cousin Nannie" was an eye-roller and breath-taker. Cousin Nannie's father had a favorite pear tree in the backyard. One year, it bore but one fruit. "Anyone who picks it," he announced to his family, "gets the licking of his life." Nannie watched and waited until the pear was ripe and ready to eat. Then she climbed a low fence near the tree and ate all around the core and left it hanging on its twig.

"Did she get spanked?" I would ask each time.

"No," Grandmother would answer. "Her father had said anyone who *picks* the pear gets a licking. And, of course, he had to keep his word."

When I was about ten or eleven, Grandmother decided storytelling was over for her grandchildren. The end was pure Grandmother Johnson.

"Tell us a story, Grandmother," Ellen, Paula, and I begged when she visited one weekend. Ellen and Paula lived around the corner from me, and we often slept at each other's house when Grandmother came to see us.

"One autumn, when I was a little girl," she began, "we

worked all day to fill the big barn with corn. In the morning a locust came and carried off a grain of corn. The next day another locust took another grain of corn, and that afternoon another locust took away another grain of corn."

"What happened," I butted in, "when the grain was all gone?"

"Another locust came and took away another grain of corn." That went on until we gave up and went to bed. The next time we asked for a story, Grandmother smiled and said, "Another locust came and took away another grain of corn."

Ellen, Paula, and I decided the only way to get Grandmother to tell us stories again was to empty that barn. We spent one entire day repeating grandmother's phrase as we got locusts to carry off grains of corn. That night we told Grandmother the barn was empty. "Please, tell us a story."

"And then another locust came and took away another grain of corn."

My brothers carried off grains of corn for three days, reported their success, and asked Grandmother to tell them a story.

"And then another locust came and took away another grain of corn." We knew our childhood was over.

As Grandmother grew older, her eyes failed her. She would let no one give her sympathy, and most people were unaware of her condition. She walked through the rooms of her home performing old familiar chores. She sewed aprons for the church bazaar by feeling her way along the hems with her fingers.

What she lacked in vision she made up in insight. One

afternoon when I was home from college, I stopped by to visit. Grandmother looked up as I came in the room.

"Jean," she said. "Why aren't you wearing stockings?" She knew me well. I wasn't.

Now that I am eighty-two, I recall her last great axiom: "The young may die, the old must." Then she would add, "So you might as well grow old pleasurably. You'll only do it once." And she did just that. She made each meal a work of art with doilies, silverware, china, fresh flowers, and good conversation whenever possible. She enjoyed keeping herself neat and stylishly dressed and always smelled of lavender sachets. She brushed her rich auburn hair each morning with endless strokes. Although she wished it would turn white, it never did.

Her sons and daughters, as well as her grandchildren, were faithful letter writers. Once a week we wrote home from wherever we were, describing in great detail what we were doing and seeing. The letters were circulated around the family and came to rest in Grandmother's desk at 509 Duke Street. One of the great pleasures of her old age was to have someone reread these family letters written from China, Japan, India, even Maine and Wyoming. "The history of a family," my mother called them.

Family to Grandmother came before all else. It was a ring that no outsiders entered, not even the in-laws. They were close, but not "really family." We laughed at her exclusiveness, but we knew she meant it. Only children and their children were "clan."

In her last years, Grandmother held on to her children

and grandchildren through the telephone. Calls from Alexandria to D.C., where Mother and Aunt Polly lived, were five cents for five minutes, so Grandmother kept a clock by the phone. Did she see it? Did she hear it? No one knows, but at the end of five minutes, often in the middle of a sentence, she would hang up. If she was teaching us a lesson in frugality, she managed to do it. Not only do my brothers and cousins watch the clock as we talk, but for years we all called one another only after six or on Sunday, when the rates were lower.

This dramatic lady was not without a great story to end her life. At ninety-six her heart was failing. She retired to her bedroom. During the day, Grandmother's daughters and her daughter-in-law took turns at her side, and Aunt Catherine, who lived with her, took over at the end of her workday. On the last day of her life, Martha, the daughter-in-law, was with her.

"I watched her fight for life all day," Aunt Martha recalled. "Then the door opened and Catherine walked in."

"Catherine," Grandmother called softly, "is that you?"

"Yes, Mother, I'm home."

Family was with her, and Mary Agnes Aitcheson Johnson closed her eyes. She never turned around and made her bed again.

THINGS TO REMEMBER 1940

Sayings from Mary Agnes Aitcheson Johnson's little hand-written books to her grandchildren.

"Truth is mighty and must prevail."

"Things we most dread seldom happen."

"If you want anything done well, do it yourself."

"One is seldom sorry for having said too little."

"Take care of your reputation, your character will take care of itself."

"Money makes the mare go."

"Good manners is consideration for others."

"One lie leads to another."

"There's no accounting for taste, as the old woman said when she kissed the cow."

"You can't get a clean bird out of a dirty nest."

"Always face the music."

"Whatever is, is right."

"A promise made is a debt unpaid."

"To the pure all things are pure."

"Charity begins at home."

"Absence makes the heart grow fonder."

"Out of sight, out of mind."

"O wad some power the giftie gie us to see ourselves as others see us."

"Never spend all you make."

"Nothing succeeds like success."

"When poverty comes in the door, love flies out the window."

"If you look for trouble, you are likely to find it."

"Blood is thicker than water."

"He who fights and runs away, lives to fight another day."

"You get out of the world just what you put into it."

"If you don't look for gratitude, you will not be disappointed."

"Man proposes. God disposes."

"Let not the sun go down upon your wrath."

"A fool can give advice. It's a wise man who takes it."

"It is better to bear the ills we know than to fly to ills we know not of."

"We learn most through our mistakes."

"Don't ride a willing horse to death."

"There are more flies caught by sugar than by vinegar."

"What has been said can never be unsaid."

"Self-preservation is the first law of nature."

"Character is above intellect."

AUTHOR'S NOTE

Now I am a grandmother. I thrill to warm little bodies and wistful eyes. I come running at the sound of needful cries. I tell stories and occasionally stop the giggles with Grandmother's permissive cure.

I also see what Grandmother saw, something that had eluded me until I became a grandmother—the magnetism of family.

My first grandchild, Rebecca, awakened me to this. She

was about four months old. I was visiting her for the second time since her birth and eagerly took her, crying, from her tired mother. I cradled her in my arms. She stopped sobbing and looked up at me. Her blue eyes studied my face. *We belong to each other* passed between us.

In that magic moment, I thought of a scientific experiment that had astounded me. Four families of pollywogs were color-marked when they hatched from their egg masses. They were then separated and stirred up in a big tank. Within a short time, the blues found the blues, the reds the reds, etc. If lowly pollywogs know their own kin, I said to myself, this marvelously complex human baby certainly knows hers.

So did my one-year-old grandson, Sammy, down from the Arctic for our first meeting. He managed the front steps on hands and feet and dove into my arms with no introduction.

And little Hunter, now four, stared at me at our first meeting with a secret smile that said, *You and I are connected.* I looked back and smiled, *Yes, we are.* Grandmother Johnson put it this way: "Birds of a feather flock together."

Although I live far from my grandchildren—I am in New York, and they are in Maryland, Alaska, and California— this magnetism erases the distances. My grandchildren and I flock together over the phone, through e-mail, with letters, books, and paintings. When we meet and travel to far-flung places, as we do quite often, my concern about living so far from them dissolves into a Grandmother Johnson saying: "Whatever is, is right."

Agreeing with that, I make up a saying for myself: "Whatever is right, is inspiration." I have written five books inspired by my far-flung grandchildren: *Dear Rebecca, Winter Is Here; Arctic Son; Yes, Katy, the Volcano Is a Girl; Morning, Noon, and Night;* and *Everglades.*

Will I wait for the door to open and a voice to call, "Mom,"—"Grammy," perhaps "Great-Grammy"—"I am home"? I think I will.

BEVERLEY NAIDOO

Granny Was a Gambler

I have only two firsthand memories of Granny. In the first, I am not sure how old I am. Maybe four or five. I am sitting with my brother, Paul, in the back of our car. We are waiting. He draws in his sketchbook while I look at my book. It is hot and we squabble a bit. Waiting always seems to take so long. The car is parked close to a wire fence. On the other side there are rows of little bungalows. Granny is inside one of them. Or maybe she's inside the white walls of a building farther away, shaded by tall blue gum trees. Mommy has taken Granny a plate of her favorite fish, and Daddy has gone with her. It's Saturday. Visiting day. If we are good while we wait, we will be taken somewhere afterward for a treat.

At last there are our parents coming back through the gates. I hang out of the window. Suddenly, I hear a voice calling us from the other side of the fence. In the distance, between far-off bungalows, a tiny woman in a pale gown is waving. Is she coming toward us? She has the same gray wavy hair and the same small face as Granny in Mommy's photo album. I have never seen Granny in person, so I am not sure it is her. I wave back, shyly. Mommy and Daddy wave and climb into the car. We drive away. Granny turns into a dot.

Did we ask why we couldn't enter the place behind the wire fence? Probably we were told that Granny wasn't well . . . hadn't been well for a long time. Perhaps Mommy added that it would be too upsetting for Granny to see us. We should wait until we got older and Granny got better. Then we could meet her.

We got older, but Granny did not get better. In time, I came to understand that she wasn't physically sick. Granny was mentally ill. Apparently she lived in a separate world in her head. Mommy said it was something to do with the shock of her husband dying when he was still young, and then losing all her money. She didn't add any details and I didn't ask. Granny was ill and I didn't really think much about her. My brother was away at boarding school for most of the year, and we rarely saw Mommy's two uncles, so the idea of family members being separated didn't seem particularly odd.

My brother and I didn't see Granny again until shortly before she died. I was nearly nineteen, already in my second year at my South African university, when my mother finally took me to meet her. This was my second and only other memory of Granny. And it was our first and last proper meeting. By this time Granny had cancer and looked even more waiflike than in my first memory. She was now in Sterkfontein Hospital—"strong fountain," in English. It had a grim reputation as a hospital in which people were "put away." Why was Granny in a place that looked and felt like a fortress and where the nurses spoke more Afrikaans than English? Sterkfontein was in Krugersdorp, a white Afrikaner town, that felt stern and strange to me, an English-speaking girl from the more diverse city of Johannesburg.

My journey to and from the hospital with my mother must have been full of silences and unasked questions. I don't know why I didn't ask, or demand, to know more. I was old enough to know that there was a history here that had been buried. Perhaps I didn't ask because, by this time, I was already becoming deeply troubled by how we lived, and this absorbed me. I had begun to question the racism that was passed on to most young white people in ways that made it seem normal and that shaped our daily lives. I was beginning to understand what apartheid actually meant. It was a crime against other human beings, like Nazi crimes in Europe. Furthermore, we were all part of it unless we did something about it. My brother, who was older than me, had led the way for me in beginning to break away from racist ways of seeing and being. By getting involved in resistance to apartheid, he was already living in a very different world from that of our parents. Partly in his footsteps, even though I was still living at home in our small apartment, I had begun to separate myself from my parents and how they lived. Perhaps I felt there were enough arguments already, and it wasn't worth trying to dig into family history that my mother found painful. This is the only way I can explain why I remember so little about my visit to Granny and why a shroud lies over my mind around her death, four days after my nineteenth birthday.

I think my parents must have attended her funeral on their own. Did my mother want it private that way? It is quite possible. Or did she ask me if I wanted to attend and did I say, "No thank you"? Surely not. But . . . a little part of my brain is not absolutely certain that I wasn't actually there. Could I have forgotten? Or is this my mind playing tricks, tantalizing me with the thought that I might have been there? But surely I *should* remember if I went to my own grandmother's funeral? The questions scold me now: How can I not know? This is just one of the holes not only in my own memory but that are part of Granny's story itself—as Mommy told it to me.

In 1965, two years after Granny died, I left South Africa for England. I had been imprisoned without charge and had attended my brother's trial. Over the next twenty years my parents managed four short visits to see me and my brother—who had also come into exile in England after jail, torture, banning, and house arrest. They came, as well, to see their grandchildren. We kept in touch mainly by letters. They knew that we were still busy with work against apartheid but we usually only wrote and spoke about everyday matters. It was easier that way. Occasionally, one of us slipped up and a mine would explode underfoot. It was hard work then to restore calm and show that we could still love one another despite the terrible gulf created by apartheid that we would never bridge.

I never asked Mommy to tell me more about Granny, nor

did she volunteer. Now, more than fifty years after glimpsing a distant figure who was Granny—behind a wire fence—I am trying to make sense of the extraordinary tale my mother told us as children. I realize how full of holes it is. I feel as if I am trying to catch water with a sieve. There are many questions that I should have asked my mother. I never asked them as a child, when I was too accepting. I never asked them as an adult—and now it is too late.

Here is what I have been able to piece together, from different sources: memories of stories my mother told me when I was a child, packets of sepia-colored postcards and photographs, a little book of handwritten poems, an address book, and—most valuable of all—diaries that my mother kept in her late teens and early twenties. For years I left these tucked away in the boxes sent from Johannesburg after her death. But, at last, I have been reading them, hoping to fill in some of the holes about Granny, including her relationship with Mommy. . . .

Granny was a gambler. That was the story I carried in my head from childhood. Mommy told me that Granny had lost her money at casinos on the French Riviera—Monte Carlo, Cannes, Nice, and all those places that sounded so exotic to a child thousands of miles away at the other end of Africa. Both Granny's parents had emigrated from Eastern Europe to England in the second half of the nineteenth century. Although anti-Semitism thrived in England, in Russia there were actual pogroms against Jews. I don't know whether my great-grandparents were directly caught up in these or whether they simply believed life would be better in England. Mommy's father, Israel Levison, was born in London, and Granny, whose name was Rachel Jacobs, was born in Birmingham or Manchester. I don't know when or where they married but being young and white, they took advantage of the opportunities and privilege the British Empire gave them and set off for South Africa. He left all his family behind in England but Granny's two brothers, Sol and Abe, chose to emigrate there too.

I think my grandfather may have trained to be a teacher but he became an auctioneer and later started a classy men's dress shop in Johannesburg instead. He gave it his own surname, Levison, and it is still there today, though it is no longer in the family. In Mommy's favorite picture of him, he is sitting in an armchair in their garden on a fine South African winter day in June 1927. His face is sharp, chiseled and handsome. You can see he was a snappy dresser: bow tie, a light jacket and waistcoat, stylish socks with a pattern of diamonds, and glossy shoes. Gunner, the family Alsatian, sits alert at his feet. Master and dog share an air of command. Mommy said that her father had treated Granny like a precious doll. But soon after that picture was taken, when he was only in his mid-forties, my grandfather died. Granny and Mommy, who was an only child, were devastated. Like many women of her generation and social class, Granny had never had to do anything except perhaps give a few instructions to servants. She had never had to handle money—my grandfather had just given her whatever she needed. Granny was at a loss, and

Mommy said someone (she would never say who) unwisely advised Granny to sell the shop. Granny listened and sold it. Taking enough money to live comfortably and investing the rest, she set off with my mother, then eighteen, for Europe. They sailed from Cape Town in 1929.

They visited London first, but it wasn't long before they began touring the continent. They traveled to Paris, Geneva, Milan, and by the end of 1930 were settled into Nice in the south of France. Mommy kept packets of little sepia postcards from all these places, neatly wrapped in special paper and embossed with the name of each place they visited. When I was growing up, those grainy pictures of faraway European cities with centuries-old buildings seemed musty and remote to me, a child from an African city that was barely seventy years old.

In their early days in Nice, it seems that both mother and daughter were captivated. In her "Jimmy Book," as Mommy called her diary, she raves about "the magic" of the Mediterranean Sea and light. Frequent pleasures included Granny visiting the casino and Mommy going dancing. Granny loved shopping. Dressmakers and hatmakers appear in Mommy's list of addresses. They must have looked as elegant as inhabitants of the grand Hotel Negresco, although they lived somewhere much simpler themselves. They steered clear of young men looking for women with money, but both mother and daughter were flattered by an attractive young man's attention.

Mommy records one incident in a casino at Monte Carlo when Granny "went to her doom with a fatal glint in her eye."

Mommy stayed on the terrace outside, listening to music. Granny was late, and Mommy built up a temper waiting for her. However when Granny emerged, she was waving three hundred francs, so Mommy forgave all. They celebrated at the Café de Paris, where Granny told her that a good-looking Swedish boy, accompanied by his guardian, had brought her luck at the casino table. Later on that night, they met the same young man, and Mommy was furious when he commented on how grown-up she looked for her age. Granny had told him that her daughter was only fifteen!

In another incident in September 1931, when they were living in a one-bedroom flat in Nice, Mommy recounts a surreal night when they were woken by the sound of strange whirring. She woke Granny by yelling. When Granny turned on the lights, they found two bats in their room. Both women were horrified, having heard Dracula tales that bats love human hair! Granny shrieked and scampered back under the bedcovers to hide. In a fit of nervous giggles, Mommy knocked at "Next Door" for help. Next Door came in his nightclothes and, with a broom, performed a ballet, pirouetting and swaying, but missing the bats. In between the broom dance, he asked Mommy whether she bathed at the Grande Bleue and was that lump in the bed her mother? When the bats were finally routed, Granny emerged and solemnly shook his hand. Their strange neighbor turned out to be a dancer from the Russian Ballet resting after a tiring season, under doctor's orders to lead a quiet life.

Mommy spoke perfect French but I doubt that Granny did. While Mommy was caught in her own whirl of social activity, what was Granny doing? Sometimes Mommy mentions her—sitting down at the beach, strolling along the Promenade des Anglais, or dining out with friends. But apart from her "usual flutter" in the casino, what did she do?

On one occasion, Mommy writes about a fluster of excitement when they were invited to be part of the crowd of extras in a film being shot on the beach at Monte Carlo. For a few days, they were each paid 100 francs a day for Mommy to splash in the water and play on the beach while Granny rested in a green hammock.

Another time, Granny met a "repulsive-looking man . . . a well-known writer" and confided that her daughter was keen on writing. He immediately suggested that he and Mommy work together. He would give Mommy his plots and she could write his stories. Mommy was excited about getting published but she soon suspected his motives and made sure he kept his distance. A few weeks later, when he told her that the stories had been turned down, she was not surprised because the work was "tripe." But Mommy still wrote that she was a failure, though she did hint at blaming Granny just a little.

The later entries in the Jimmy Books show a growing strain between mother and daughter. For instance, Granny kept a watchful eye over Mommy's potential romances and Mommy was always highly offended by Granny's suspicions. Mommy also jumped at every opportunity to act, and while Granny didn't seem to mind her dabbling, she had severe misgivings about Mommy's desire to work in the theater more permanently.

But beneath all the normal mother-daughter tensions, there are increasing hints of Granny's loneliness and of something much more seriously wrong. By June 1931, after six months in Nice, Granny had begun talking about returning home. Mommy knew they couldn't continue "floating" forever but, after the freedom of life in Europe, she had a horror of being "trapped" and stifled back in Johannesburg. It was really just a mining town. Granny would want her to marry a good Jewish husband and settle down to regular married life.

Did they argue openly, mother and daughter? Or were the battles just silent? Probably they engaged in both. Mommy writes of a drive up into the mountains to Juan-les-Pins where, despite the magnificent scenery, she had returned in a terrible mood. One of the worst, she wrote, she had ever known. She acknowledges that she "Made Mum miserable—myself more wretched than ever on realising my vile selfishness." A couple of weeks later, her tone is even more somber. She is "suddenly afraid." She feels "an inconscient haunting dread of the unknown. Mum is worrying me. She seems to be getting depressed and melancholy."

But there was an even more pressing reason for Granny's agitation. In November 1931, Mommy talks about the crash in the pound and "being afraid to spend a bean." Granny's money had been invested in shares on the Johannesburg Stock Exchange. Thousands of investors lost their savings when the global depression reached South Africa. Frightened, Granny wanted to pack up and go home but Mommy resisted. An

American woman had invited her to join her traveling theater company and she was over the moon! But Granny held out, and the American woman was jailed a couple of months later in Paris for signing checks with no money behind them. Mommy writes that she felt Fate had saved her.

Poor Granny! She must have been constantly worried about a daughter so full of ambition, impatient for success and who refused to return home and settle down. But did Granny herself really think of South Africa as "home" when she had been born in England into a family who had come from Eastern Europe? What puzzles me greatly, however, is why Mommy writes hardly at all about Granny's family in England—not even after they moved on to London in October 1932, after having toured through Spain. For the next year it seems that Granny and Mommy moved from one boardinghouse to the next. Mommy's diary entries aren't so frequent and, apart from reports of plays and outings with a few friends, I have little idea how they filled their time. Where did Granny's family live? Who were they? In Mommy's address book there is an entry marked GRANDPA—S. JACOBS in Stamford Hill, London, an area known for Orthodox Jews. Yet Mommy never mentions him in her Jimmy Books. How strange! There is only one entry about "Uncle & Aunt" (no names) taking Granny and Mommy on a summer's day-trip to Brighton. I can't help feeling that Mommy didn't tell Jimmy everything, despite her promise in the beginning that she would write only "the truth." Was Granny perhaps an outcast for not following strict Orthodox

Jewish ways? Had she broken away from a family that disapproved of her own independence of spirit? Was she looked down on because she didn't settle down to a narrow widow's life? What does Mommy mean when she writes about her "marvellous but hypocritical Mother" who insisted on "no knitting" on the Sabbath? And was Granny criticized because of Mommy's independence?

After another year Granny had still not returned to South Africa, and Mommy was still adamant about staying away. There was discord. "What a business!" Mommy writes. "Why wasn't I made a placid little cowlike girl, who is the perfect daughter, and does everything her mother tells her?" Her American friend was now in London, promising to make her dreams come true, asking Mommy to help her set up a theater school. But Granny was terrified of leaving Mommy in such a precarious career. If she was to leave her daughter behind, she at least wanted her to have a "respectable job." Mommy persisted, and in January 1934 found a vacancy at the Times Book Club in London. The club dealt with the royal family. That was good enough for Granny, and she could finally go home.

Her departure for South Africa soon afterward was traumatic. She wept profusely. While Mommy shed tears at Granny's "little, drawn face at the window," she was soon very busy and happy with her work and theater rehearsals. Granny's first letter expressed her feelings of drifting apart from her daughter. Mommy found it heartbreaking but felt she had made the right decision. She pays tribute to Granny for being "such a wonderful mother—so utterly selfless in everything she's done for me." Traveling abroad had been brilliant for Mommy, but for Granny it had been "utterly foreign . . . & lonely . . . She deserves peace & love & happiness now. . . ."

It was not to be. None of those wishes for Granny came true. Fourteen months later, Mommy received an urgent telegram calling her home. She traveled on one of the early flights across Africa in a little plane that landed in a different country each night—one of the first women, she said, to do so. The journey took a week! Back in South Africa, there was little time for Jimmy, the secret friend to whom she had once poured out her heart. Mommy arrived to find that Granny's money was now completely gone and she was indeed in a bad way. Granny clearly needed help. In February 1936, Mommy writes about "a poor uncomprehending little mother with a Nervous Breakdown—& a bleak future . . . an incurable mother condemned to perhaps a ghastly fate."

It appears that Mommy was faced with an awful decision. By August 1936, I think Granny had been put away into a nursing home for people with mental illness. My brother believes she lost her mind because of guilt. He recalls a story about Granny gambling with the stocks and shares that were invested for her and Mommy when she returned to South Africa. He thinks that Granny lost them all. Perhaps that did happen and it was too much for her to bear. But the answer doesn't completely satisfy me. There are still too many holes in Granny's story. Perhaps Granny gambled with something more than money in the choices she made in life.

In writing about Granny, I have thought about how life has a strange way of forming circles. It was in 1964, shortly after Nelson Mandela was sentenced to life imprisonment, that my brother Paul and I were arrested. Our parents were in England, having saved up for a long time to go abroad. For the second time, Mommy received an urgent telegram in England telling her to come back home immediately. When she returned with Daddy, I was, by a peculiar twist of fate, in solitary confinement in the women's prison in Krugersdorp, the same fortress town in which Granny had been locked away and died two years earlier. I didn't think about this coincidence at the time, and of course Mommy didn't mention it.

For the first time also I have thought about Granny falling into her dark place. I have begun to think about her pain. Mommy buried her own pain by not talking about it—by not talking about Granny, keeping her like a secret. Who visited her apart from Mommy? Her brothers? Any of Granny's circle that Mommy dismisses so sharply in her Jimmy Book? Surely Granny still had a voice, but who listened to her? Once she was "inside," did she lose all touch with the world outside? I thought Sterkfontein Hospital might give me some clues, but their records were all burned in a fire some years ago.

I'll probably never know the answers to these questions now—nor to the most important question of all: Why did Mommy never take us children to see Granny? Did she feel she must protect us? I feel terribly sad for Granny. However disturbed, she would have loved her grandchildren. I believe we would have loved her too. Young children accept that human beings are interestingly varied, unless they are taught otherwise. Children are not born dividing the world up according to religion, class, "race," ability, or any other set of boxes. Little children do not, by themselves, say "This person is normal" and "This person is not." These are divisions that are taught and learned. Yet life is much richer when we cross boundaries that lead us into a wider and deeper understanding of other human beings, however different.

When I held Granny's hand in her hospital bed in the dreaded Sterkfontein Hospital, I was as old as Mommy when Granny took her to Nice. I shall never forget Granny's sunken eyes dwelling on me as she lay shrunk and weak.

"So now you've brought her to me," she said to Mommy. "Now that I'm dying." Terrible, painful words. They will remain with me forever.

AUTHOR'S NOTE

As a child I cried over *Anne Frank: The Diary of a Young Girl*. My mother and grandmother were Jewish and I knew those awful events could have happened to us if we had been living in Europe. I didn't realize then that the Nazis would have got rid of Granny even if she wasn't Jewish. When Hitler talked about a "healthy" nation and a "master race," he meant there was no place for people who were weak and sick as well as those marked "racially inferior." Mentally ill people faced the same fate as Jews, Gypsies, Communists, homosexuals, and other "undesirables." Hundreds of thousands of patients in mental hospitals and disabled people were murdered by poison gas, drugs, or starvation. The mass killings began in 1939, only seven years after Granny and Mommy left Nice.

In South Africa, most white people also had the idea of being masters. Even when the two European tribes—the Afrikaners and the English—fought each other, they shared the belief that there was a ladder in life and white people should be at the top, with brown and black people far below. So while I was crying over Anne Frank 6,000 miles away, I simply didn't see that other terrible injustices were actually taking place all around me through racism. I also accepted that mentally ill people like Granny were simply locked away. I looked at my world through tinted glasses that let only some injustices stand out and not others.

I never want to wear tinted glasses like that again. I feel both sad and angry at how prejudice, of whatever kind, distorts the way people see. It stops us being able to imagine and hear one another—Jews, Christians, Muslims, Africans, Arabs, Europeans, or whoever we are. It is strange how I feel my link to Granny, especially as I have been writing about her and discovering how little I know. My imagination leaps over time. What if I had known her? Would that have made a difference? With her experience—cast out from society with her voice silenced—could I have introduced her to the different ways of seeing and being that I came to choose? Might we even have reached some kind of understanding? I shall never know.

BONNIE CHRISTENSEN

Fairy Grandmother

In childhood dreams I often flew, and it was always the same. Along an old town street, around a corner, and down the hill. On the left, with its familiar yellow-and-green shingles, was my Grammy Cole's house. Number 30 East Street in Binghamton, New York. As I flew over the crest of the hill, she'd step from the doorway into sunlight with Trixie the black-spotted terrier at her heels. Slowly I'd give in to gravity and settle into her waiting hug. The scent of freshly peeled potatoes and lilacs would rise from her apron as I closed my eyes tightly, hoping to hold the moment. That was all. If there was more to the dream I don't remember.

We spent summers at 30 East Street, my mother, sister, and I, while my father was in the Adirondacks finishing a forestry degree. The rest of the year we spent in a series of different places because we moved so often. The views from our windows, the shadows cast by streetlights across our bedroom floors, and our small circles of friends were always changing. But at Grammy Cole's things stayed the same, year after year. The carved wagon train on the sideboard, the treadle sewing machine, the Maxfield Parrish prints, everything and everybody inside, and outside, stayed the same.

All our visits bore a comfortable familiarity. We'd arrive, hug Grammy Cole, tell Trixie to stop barking, my sister and I would charge to the kitchen to see Dickie Bird, the parakeet, then race through the house looking for candy, which excited Trixie to bark even more, which made us laugh louder and run faster. When an exasperated parent shouted, "Enough!" we'd drag our suitcases upstairs to the bedroom we shared. There at the threshold we'd pause for a moment before reclaiming our familiar sagging squeaky beds. The scent of mothballs mixed with dry dusty air would rise from my pillow as I sunk my face into its chenille cover. The sameness of the room was simple bliss. The wallpaper of stylized 1930s planes and trains, the perforated metal headboards, the red wooden apple on the string that you pulled to turn on, then off, the light, were always just as we'd left them. Only one thing ever changed in that little room in all those summers—the pile of ancient *National Geographics* grew and grew. But no sooner had we chosen some promising issue to peruse than all screen doors began slamming as aunts, uncles, and cousins arrived.

"Girls, come down," my mother called. Trixie barked. My grandmother sang along to the radio, "Mr. Sandman, bring me a dream."

"Girls!!!" someone hollered.

"Two, three," hollered cousin Babby, "ready or not, here I come."

A toddler cousin cried, an uncle soothed. "Pretty boy,"

shrieked Dickie Bird at himself in the mirror. And someone laughed or maybe lots of us laughed—laughter was always ringing from here or there, the house or yard, punctuating our days and nights.

Twilight called us cousins out of the heat of the house into the dampening evening. Away from parental eyes we'd torment one another, capture fireflies in mason jars, swat mosquitoes, then finally settle on the porch steps to watch the lights, first in the houses and then in the sky, appear one by one. My star wish was always the same, and I never told anyone, but it never came true. We always went home.

On weekends the great-aunts and great-uncles would appear. They had names that sounded alike, Lee and Lena, or old-fashioned names like Zetta and Ethel. When a shiny new car pulled ever, ever so slowly to stop in front of 30 East Street, we knew it was them. Finally they'd emerge from the car, smiling and bearing miraculously large gifts. "For the kids," they'd say. "You shouldn't have," my mother would sigh. But secretly I think their giving us huge stuffed animals for no particular reason pleased her, as certainly it pleased the ancient aunts and uncles, whose own children had long since moved far away.

Grammy Cole's house was filled with large bright rooms in which cloudlike curtains billowed and whimsical figurines caught the sun. I could lollygag on the oriental carpet for hours watching patterns of light move across the ceiling until a dull tap from the attic roof or a metallic clink from the cellar reminded me of the other places, dark and mysterious.

From the age of three or four I helped in the kitchen, and sometimes Grammy Cole would ask me to go down to the cellar for a jar of pickles or jam. "Well, you did that faster than lightning!" she'd exclaim when I returned a short minute later. The truth was that I was terrified of the dark, dank cellar with its labyrinth of spiderwebs and monstrous old coal furnace; its network of enormous black tentacles and gaping fire-door mouth stood ready to grab and consume an unsuspecting child.

Then there was the attic. Up we'd climb, up and up a steep flight of narrow winding stairs. The dry, hot attic air smelled of dusty wood and was full of wasps. A single hanging bulb illuminated a lifetime's collection of treasures. My favorites were the old steamer trunks filled with bits of lace, my grand-mother's mother's tiny mutton-sleeve blouse, and a football jersey, worn by my father, blood-stained from the days before helmets.

Summer life at 30 East Street was the polar opposite of our quiet and insular fall, winter, spring lives. While our family usually lived in the country or suburbs, Grammy Cole's house was in town. Friends and relatives passed by and dropped in spontaneously, lured by the aroma of baking bread and the promise of a good laugh. There was always something to laugh about. For a week we told the story of Grandpa and the chewing gum. Of how he'd put an old glob of chewed-up gum in his ashtray and how later Trixie found it, chewed it awhile, then dropped it onto the cushion of Grandpa's favorite chair. Naturally, Grandpa sat on it, and it was a big mess both for the chair and Grandpa's pants. Grammy Cole loved to tell the story and she laughed every time.

She didn't care that there was a permanent spot on the chair. "Housecleaning will still be around long after I'm gone!" she'd say when one of us ran a finger along a dusty tabletop. I liked the clean stripe left in the dusty surface. At home there was no place to leave a mark. Dusting was done on a weekly basis.

Fun, performing, and dreaming were all more important than dusting at my grandmother's house. Grammy Cole often talked about running off with the circus, of being a trapeze lady. Even into her eighties she recited funny poems and performed parlor-trick contortions that we all begged her to teach us. Our favorite was the "human chicken," a feat that required stuffing both arms and legs into the sleeves of a cardigan sweater that would then be buttoned over her back and a feather duster tucked under the bottom button. Thus encumbered she'd strut around the room "puck-puck-pucking" like the real thing. We rolled on the floor and howled with delight.

Grammy Cole never told us to "simmer down." Things were different under her roof. When we baked molasses cookies she'd leave gobs of cookie dough in the bowl for me to clean out. She let Dickie Bird fly freely around the house or sit on the kitchen table eating the butter, preening and shedding feathers. "Pretty boy, pretty bird," she'd say to him, and he'd echo her. Later I learned she'd also taught Dickie Bird a few other phrases. On my father's first courting visit to the Cole household, Dickie Bird had landed on his shoulder. What a wonderful omen! Everyone had sighed and cooed with obvious delight, and then Dickie Bird had uttered another cute phrase Grammy Cole had taught him: "Get out of here, you bum."

Dickie Bird probably didn't like sharing my grandmother's attention any more than I did. And I had plenty of competition.

There were twelve of us Cole grandchildren altogether. Ten lived nearby. My feeling was they should just butt out during the summer, since they had Grammy Cole to themselves all the rest of the year. But I always loved it when they showed up with all their high jinks, jokes, and laughter; they were Grammy Cole's apprentices. And, after all, there were times I had Grammy Cole all to myself.

The least fun was when she took me "calling." She'd wear a hat with feathers, and we always took food or flowers to those fragile women, some of whom I later realized were housebound. Some had been Grammy's childhood friends, some she'd known since the Great Depression, but they all talked about boring things and people I didn't know. "Bless her soul," they'd say. Or, "Goodness, I'll be!" Then they laughed when nothing seemed funny. I sat up straight and smiled, swung my feet, stifled yawns, stared out the window, and reminded myself that this was good because neither Tina, my sister, nor my cousins were there. Just me and Grammy Cole.

After calling we'd stroll to the playground or on special occasions go to a movie matinee. We saw *Sleeping Beauty*, *Pinocchio*, and our favorite, *Lady and the Tramp*, in the Cameo Theatre, chomping popcorn and whispering secretly. The shock of emerging from the theater into the midday summer sun always knocked me back on my heels. Then Grammy Cole would take my hand and we'd head off to my grandfather's small grocery store. Inside was cool and dark. I'd cruise ever so slowly by the candy counter, trying to look wistful and deprived, hoping someone would take pity and hand me some Necco wafers or Red Hots.

Besides when we went calling, I had Grammy Cole all to myself on the garden porch. The porch, on the back of the house, was cluttered and dark and smelled of dirt and dead leaves. There we planted seeds in little clay pots, and when at last the tiny sprouts emerged we'd declare it a "wonder"—every time. Outside we set seedlings and clipped armfuls of peonies. "They smell delicious, but don't sniff too hard," Grammy would warn. "You're liable to get an ant up your nose."

Sometimes I used the little trowel to plant peach pits or watermelon seeds in the backyard. I was like a dog burying bones here and there. She didn't mind. When our work was done we'd be covered in dirt, our fingernails encrusted. We'd grin and tell each other, "Good job!"

Summer slipped by with lightning storms and Popsicles, fireflies and questions about the meaning of honesty. Hammock fights, dusk tag, and cuts and bruises. Baking and planting and calling and matinees at the Cameo. Ironing while we watched wrestling on TV. Eventually a trip to the shoe store and new leather shoes, red school shoes that smelled wonderful when you lifted the box lid but were also a sad sign that summer was coming to an end.

We'd leave in early morning while dew still clung to the

grass and just-delivered milk bottles and newspapers waited beside kitchen doors. Grammy Cole waved good-bye from the curb as Trixie sauntered back to the house. I watched her wave and wave, watching us drive away until we crested the hill and disappeared. The tablets of malted milk she'd given me for "an unhappy stomach" would begin to stick to my sweating palm and the prickly car seat irritated my bare legs. All of this plus the growing heat of the day set the tone for the trip. My sister and I fought constantly. We rolled our eyes and snickered at our parents' threat: "If you don't stop that fighting, we'll leave you by the side of the road." The fact that the threat was truly ridiculous was the only thing Tina and I agreed on during the entire ten-hour drive. Why not argue? What did we have to look forward to? We were on the road back to school, back home. And because we moved often, our house, our street, was forever changing, while summer and 30 East Street remained the same.

The winter I turned eleven, everything changed. My grandfather died. My father accepted a new job. We moved again. That summer we didn't visit 30 East Street.

It wasn't easy moving from a small college town in the Appalachian Mountains to the suburbs of Washington, D.C. I began sixth grade feeling like the chubby new kid with the hillbilly accent. My teeth stuck out all over the place, I was the teacher's pet in math, and the only thing I could talk about was books. The cool girls wore lipstick, talked about songs like "Palisades Park," and went to parties with boys. Although there were other students new to the class, they'd arrived from places like Thailand, Brazil, or Switzerland. Their fathers were army colonels or executives with the World Bank, and one father eventually became a U.S. president. I'd arrived from West Virginia and my father was a forester. "You mean your dad's a tree doctor?" they'd say with a smirk. I didn't correct them.

Volleyball was their favorite sport. They could hit the ball over the net as easily as they could charm us all with their perfect smiles. Unfortunately, my first instinct, when a ball comes hurtling at my head, has always been to duck. I was the last to be picked for the volleyball team—always.

Grammy Cole wrote me letters: "Made an apple pie last night. Jud and Mart came down today for lunch and later Lee and Zetta dropped in. They asked me about you and your new school. I hope you like it. I'm sure you do. Love and xxxxx." I couldn't bear to write her the truth. I still dreamed of being at 30 East Street, where I was a sort of princess. When Grammy Cole brushed my hair she'd call the cowlicks "crowns" and tell me that having two "crowns" meant someday I'd live in two kingdoms. How could I tell her that I was barely existing in one? Certainly she'd be disappointed. I hoped she'd assume I was just too busy to write. And there was always the remote possibility that things would improve a bit, that eventually I'd have something positive to report.

At night I listened to far-off radio stations and dreamed of getting a horse. Though I didn't believe in Santa Claus, I still entertained the possibility that there was a monster, or more likely an escaped convict, seeking refuge beneath my bed. Every morning I woke up feeling sick.

We lived through the Cuban missile crisis, ducking and

covering every day, and I realized that I'd never have a horse in the suburbs. I began campaigning for a parakeet like Dickie Bird. My campaign was brutal and relentless, but the answer was always the same: No.

One night at dinner, my father cleared his throat for a family announcement. This usually meant we'd be moving again. "Good," I thought. "This is one move that'll actually make me happy." But it wasn't a move my father was announcing, and the news took me far beyond the realm of happiness. Grammy Cole was coming to live with us in just a few weeks. Elation. I couldn't sleep, didn't eat. I twitched and tapped and nearly burst with anticipation.

I'm sure she was wearing a hat when she arrived, and I'm sure she was carrying Dickie Bird's cage with its embroidered cover, though I wasn't there to see it. That day I ran home from school and there she was, drinking Postum and folding kitchen towels like she'd been there forever. She had her own bedroom and bath on the first floor, and suddenly it was filled with furniture and objects from 30 East Street. It was sometimes sad to think of strangers living there now. What would happen to all the peach pits I'd planted in the backyard? And where would I fly in my dreams? But now I had Grammy Cole all to myself, or I'd only have to share her with Tina. Heaven.

Everyday after that I'd run home to Grammy Cole and tell her about school. We'd walk around the garden, pick roses, then sit on the porch while we removed the thorns. She'd tell me things about herself. Some of the things I'd heard before, some were new. She said one of her major regrets was losing the opportunity to ride an elephant because a friend coerced her into riding the camel instead. The friend insisted on the camel because "it was more biblical."

Often we'd look at slides of different countries in her View-Master and dream. We waited on the porch, during long summer thunderstorms, counting seconds from thunder to lightning. Sometimes she'd let me sit in her cushioned rocking chair while we sketched pictures.

When my father complained that I used too much salt on my food, she defended me, blaming the salt shaker, and she never noticed when we fed the dog under the table. My father seemed amused by her perspective. There was a mountain of admiration and love between the two of them, though I don't think they ever spoke of it.

Grammy Cole's role in the household was initially to look after my sister and me. "Don't fight," she'd tell us. "There's nothing to fight about, and your mother's been working hard all day." It was true. My mother spent whole days cleaning the big house, gardening, painting rooms, making curtains, planning meals. She took her job as homemaker seriously. But I didn't see why Grammy Cole was protecting her. Sometimes we had to be reminded that my mother was, after all, Grammy Cole's little girl.

Eventually Grammy Cole decided to take over more of the household chores, including the ironing. Underwear, handkerchieves, and every sheet and pillowcase—all had to be ironed. As she ironed, the smell of steaming cotton permeated the air, reminding me of 30 East Street. I imagined how difficult it must have been to leave. Her letters had always been full of cooking and baking and comings and goings: "Leonard came and took me to his house. Jani gave me a perm, then Leonard brought me home. I sure have a nice family." I looked back over those letters and thought about how quiet and unspontaneous our house was compared with 30 East Street and its endless chain of colorful characters.

That winter I had bronchitis and needed a steam tent. Grammy Cole insisted I stay in her room. The windows steamed over and droplets slid down the panes as she read aloud *Great Expectations* and then *Oliver Twist*.

Back at school I relaxed. Nothing seemed so bad or important. Gradually things improved. My drawings were chosen for the student art show, and I was asked to be on a committee to organize Parents' Day. Because my father couldn't attend, Grammy Cole took his place. She and my mom were the last to arrive. Some of my classmates made faces. Afterward one of them said, "Why does your grandmother have purple hair?"

"She doesn't," I said. "It's just some blue stuff she puts on it to make it brighter." It went on like that until I walked away. I really didn't care what they thought.

That afternoon Grammy Cole met me at the door. "I enjoyed meeting all your friends!" She smiled. Her eyes, magnified by thick glasses, were huge and bright. And, yes, her hair was purple, but, no, I didn't care. I thought about Christmas and how we always borrowed her glasses to look at the haloed colored lights magnified in those thick lenses.

Grammy Cole lived with us for two years. Then it was time to move again, and she decided to return to Binghamton.

It wouldn't be 30 East Street, because the big old house had been sold. But there was a comfortable apartment nearby, where all her friends and her "nice family" could drop in any-time.

She told me this herself. We were in her room. I was in her rocking chair, and she was sitting on the bed looking out the window at the gray sky.

"You'll be fine," she said. "You'll make lots of nice new friends, and we'll write lots of letters." I tried not to let the tears forming in my eyes overflow, but in the next instant I could feel them running down my neck. I looked out the window, too. The rusty top bar of the swing set was lined with snow, but on one end the snow had been knocked off by a purple finch.

"Purple finch," I said, wiping my nose with the back of my hand. "Did you ever mark off 'purple finch' in your bird book?" She took my hand and we sat in the silence of twilight until the gray sky gave way to a gently falling snow.

The empty space her departure left in my life seemed entirely and forever unfillable. But now I realize it's comfortably occupied by my daughter—so much like Grammy Cole in so many ways. I listen carefully when Em tells me about her flying dreams, and once dared to wonder if someday a future grandchild might dream of flying to my house. My house, with its Maxfield Parrish print and oriental rug, the old wooden egg bucket, perfume bottles, and the picture of Grammy Cole flexing her muscles—all once part of 30 East Street. So many tangible treasures.

And the intangible?

My great good fortune that Grammy Cole came so fully into my life when she did, and that I have so much of her philosophy to carry lightly with me.

Whenever I manage a laugh during hard times or go to the county fair instead of cleaning house, when I spend money I don't have to hear glorious music or fly off to a foreign country wearing a silly hat, when I get the urge to watch wrestling while ironing and my daughter's friends secretly roll their eyes at me—for all this and much more, I have only Grammy Cole to thank. And I do.

AUTHOR'S NOTE

This is my second author's note. In the first, written a year ago, I spoke of Grandmother Christensen, the tragedies she'd faced and her strengths. Grammy Cole's life, in contrast, seemed easy and carefree—the tricks of time and selective memory erased all but the most idyllic impressions.

When I got my "call" six months ago, other memories of Grammy Cole came back to me. She was the only woman I'd ever known who'd had a mastectomy. I remembered finding little blue flannel bra pads in the laundry after she'd moved in with us, my mother's explanation for what they were, and Grammy Cole's theory, that, "it was better it had happened to her than to someone who couldn't handle it." Could that have been true? Having cancer never seemed to bother her. She accepted it as part of life. Now I wonder if her special zest and enthusiasm might not have been at least partially influenced by the cancer.

Certainly facing cancer, having the mastectomy, has changed my life. Through it all I held on to the feeling that Grammy Cole was with me, and that if she could do it, I could, too. Eventually, the fear and anxiety of having cancer gave way to a sense of freedom and an acute appreciation for small everyday moments. I wish my grandmother were here so we could talk about the silver lining phenomenon and laugh.

And when friends say, "You've handled this so well!" I always think of my role model, and wonder how many more unexpected lessons she has in store for me. I imagine and hope that, since she lived to be eighty-four, there will be many.

JI-LI JIANG

To My Nai Nai

I jerk awake, sobbing, soaked with sweat, my heart tight with pain.

For a moment, I forget where I am. In total darkness and absolute silence, I wait, and I remember. I am in my California apartment, thousands of miles from Shanghai, my hometown.

Nai Nai, I saw you in my dreams again. You were sweeping our alley. It was afternoon. A summer storm was coming, dark and windy. Your white shirt shook like a sail blown by a swirling gale, and your hair covered your face as you struggled to gather all the trash into the dustpan.

Then three children passed by. Seeing you, a landowner's widow being punished, made to sweep the alley, they approached you, eager to show some revolutionary power. A-ming, the meanest one, whose father was a policeman, kicked the dustpan out of your hand, scattering the dust you had gathered. You said nothing, but only looked at him. He angrily spit the cigarette from his mouth and then roughly pushed you. You fell to the ground.

The room is so dark and quiet. I hear only my own breath. Looking at the blank ceiling, I can't go back to sleep. I keep remembering many things about you, Nai Nai. So many things . . .

Some people said you had a *bitterfate*. Your mother died in a fire when you were a girl. Your father married you to a man you had never met, who was quite sick and lived in Shanghai, a thousand miles from your hometown, Tianjin. Your husband died eight years later. To protect your only son, who was seven years old, you decided not to remarry. For the next twenty years, you raised him on your own.

Then Dad graduated from college, married, and had three children, and you willingly took over the family burden. You did the cooking, shopping, and cleaning. You took care of us children. You made our shoes and clothes. You managed our family's limited income and resources by "splitting every penny in two," as you often said.

Your life was never easy, Nai Nai. Yet you never lost your passion for life or your honorable character.

When you were five years old, in accordance with Chinese tradition, your parents had your feet bound. Growing up with a pair of three-inch feet was considered the height of beauty for Chinese women, and most girls back then had this torture imposed on them for life. But you fought hard until your mother finally unbound your feet and relieved you of the extreme pain.

You also learned to read and write at a time when few girls went to school. In 1914, you went to the Teacher's Normal

School and became a teacher yourself! And then, while raising Dad on your own, you helped to found Xin-er Elementary School and became its first vice principal. Many times, when I walked with you through the streets of our neighborhood, your former students, people Dad's age, stopped us to bow to you and said respectfully, "How are you, Teacher Cao?" I was so proud to stand beside you!

Nai Nai, in my childhood memory, you never complained or showed bitterness. Your face was always kind, your voice always soft, your heart always open and loving. You embraced life as it came to you and made the most out of it. Do you know how much you taught us all by your example?

I still cherish the last picture I took of you before you got sick. It is a blurred black-and-white two-by-two–inch print. You are sitting in front of the French window on the little bamboo-made chair, wearing the white cotton shirt you made. Your back is hunched, your head is bent low so your beautiful features don't quite show, and your old amber reading glasses are perched on your nose. You are picking little dirt-grits from the uncooked rice, completely absorbed in this simple task. Nai Nai, this image of you is forever carved in my memory.

Throughout my life in China, you sat in the same spot, the same chair, year after year, picking dirt-grits from the rice, scraping mud from the vegetables, mincing beef, knitting, sewing, never idle, always tirelessly working, always sweetly giving.

When did you ever think of your own needs?

Nai Nai, do you remember the cotton shoes you made for us? Piece by piece you pasted countless tiny cloth remnants on a flat board to make buckram, humming sometimes in your soft tone. Then you cut the dried buckram into many pieces, which you shaped and stitched together, pricking your finger with the needle from time to time, to fit our small feet. How much heart and soul you wove into these "thousand-stitch shoes." How carelessly we wore them out!

But your knitting impressed me the most of all the tasks you did. You made sweaters for everyone in our family when we had no money to buy them. When the sweaters wore out, you unraveled them and drew them back into yarn, which you carefully washed and steamed. This "new yarn," some parts still thick and some parts thin, you knitted into sweaters again. You used the different parts in different ways, so patiently and carefully, using the most useless yarn to reinforce the thinnest areas of these "new" sweaters. I watched with such admiration as you made one sweater after another. The finished products were so perfect no one would ever imagine our beautiful sweaters were made of old wear-and-tear yarn. We proudly wore the same old yarn in different sweaters, reknitted in different patterns and mixed with different colors, year after year.

But although you were always busy, working constantly, never having time for yourself, you were always there for us. With Dad and Mom usually at work, you were the one with whom we played and laughed and ate, and to whom we came when we cried. We often went to sleep hearing the sound of your lullaby. I remember how you didn't sleep for three nights when we three children all had chicken pox at once. You held us, humming to us to lessen our discomfort. I remember how we came home from school each day and showed you the songs or dances we had learned. You sat in front of us, knitting and smiling, swinging slightly to and fro with our rhythm. Do you remember how we tickled you to make you sing along with us? And how sweet you sounded, singing with your heavy Tianjin accent and unsteady pitch, wagging your head just like us as we sang with you.

Even all our friends loved you. When they came to our house in the afternoons to do homework, you crinkled your smiling eyes, softly greeting them as "little friends" in your Tianjin dialect, treating them as honored guests. They said you were the kindest grandma they had ever met.

And Nai Nai, do you remember your funny bed, our favorite place for storytelling? With our family of six people in a one-room apartment, you slept most of the time on a wooden frame strung with crisscross coir rope on top of the bathtub. We removed it, of course, when we needed to take our baths. Your small unusual bed became our playground. We all loved to crowd on it—you, me, Ji-yong, and Ji-yun— while you knitted or sewed our clothes. After we had enough laughter, tickling you, playing with your half-bound feet and your long earlobes, we would listen to the daily children's story on the radio or you would read us a book. We grew so absorbed by the stories we heard that we often forgot if we were hungry or thirsty or needed to pee, until our legs went to sleep. Mom often wondered why the crisscross rope on your wooden-frame bed got loose so fast. She didn't know it was a four-person bed!

Oh, those were our happy times. Although we had few material things, we were content because we had never lacked love from you and Dad and Mom.

But then the Cultural Revolution came, and Dad was detained as a political enemy in his company's "cowshed"—the makeshift prison that every workplace had. We were not allowed to visit him for months, and we didn't know what they were doing to him. Sometimes we didn't even know whether he was alive or dead. From the stress and working so hard, Mom fell sick and often passed out. But she was denied sick leave and was told to lie down at the back of the store where she worked if she couldn't stand up. Our home was searched twice by the revolutionaries, and they took almost everything we owned. We ended up with no tables, no chairs, and no beds. And you, Nai Nai, at the age of seventy-four, who had helped so many and never done any harm to anyone, were forced to become a street sweeper with a "rotten" political record. You were labeled as one of the "ghosts and monsters," the so-called enemies of the people. You were "struggled" against at neighborhood meetings and forced to perform public self-criticisms. You had to go out twice a day for more than a year to sweep our neighborhood street as a punishment for being the widow of a landowner who had died more than thirty years earlier.

Yet, despite all of this, you never yielded to pressure, nor stopped loving and giving to other people.

I recall how for years you wrote letters, giving courage to your friend Teacher Qi, who had become an outcast in her community because of her son's politics. You even sent her a couple of yuan from time to time, which was all you could save. Even in the most difficult time for our family, you never stopped writing your calm, kind words to her in your shaky handwriting, despite the political danger to you. You knew that her letters were probably read by her Neighborhood Party Committee. Yet you never stopped writing her until she passed away.

So many things our family learned by being with you, seeing how you lived in good times and bad. You never judged people by their status, their power, or their money. You applied the same principles to all, treating others as equal to yourself. I remember how you often taught us, "If you succeed, *don't forget* who you are; if you fail, *remember* who you are."

Nai Nai, I am sure you remember what happened to me in the fifth grade, the low point of my life. I began having mysterious pains and trouble with my joints and was diagnosed with severe arthritis. The doctor said I had to stop all physical activities and stay home from school for one year. I was so frightened, Nai Nai, that I cried and couldn't eat or sleep for days. What would I do without school, my friends, and all the fun activities I was involved in? I felt awful. Dad and Mom talked to me and encouraged me each day. But you didn't say much. Instead, you began to go out for several hours a day almost every day for the next few weeks. When you came home, hot and exhausted, your legs were sometimes so swollen that you could hardly climb the stairs.

Then, one afternoon, I walked into our room and you put down the sweater you were knitting and motioned me to come to you. You touched my braids softly and looked into my eyes and said, "Upset, right? Maybe scared, too? I know, sweetie, I know. If I were you, I would feel the same." You sighed and pressed my head tightly to your bosom. "But remember, sweetie, just like the weather, sunny, rain, storm, everyone, every single being will have difficulties or failures in life, just like you have now. When that happens, the most important thing is how you deal with it."

You picked up a piece of paper from the table. "I found this folk remedy prescription for your illness, but . . ." You paused and grinned, studying my face. "It needs a lot of courage." You waited for my response.

"What is it?" I murmured.

"A bunch of Chinese herbs. We need to boil them in a big basin and put it underneath your body so the steam heats your ill joints, while you bathe in the sun in the hottest days of the summer for twenty-seven days."

Nai Nai, we did it. We actually did it. For twenty-seven days, every day at noon I stretched out on our balcony under the scorching sun, my head and back on one chair, my feet on another, and my lower back and legs suspended in between. Then you put a big basin of herb medicine you had cooked for hours under my suspended body. I was "cooked" each day between the hot sun above me and the steaming medicine beneath me that raised blisters on my backside more than once. Often I couldn't keep my back straight for very long and it would begin to sag toward the floor. But immediately my back would bounce back straight, almost by itself, to get away from the heat of the burning steam.

Remember how many times I moaned, grumbled, twisted, whined, and whimpered? It was almost unbearable for an eleven-year-old girl. But you, Nai Nai, kept telling me to clench my teeth and hold on while you continually wiped my tears and sweaty body with a cold towel and held my hand tightly. You gave me the courage I needed. From time to time, you even sat down on the floor and used your own hands to support my back and keep it straight. I saw the wrinkles on your face become tiny rivers of sweat as your white shirt became slowly drenched and stuck to your body.

You tended me this way for twenty-seven days, Nai Nai. You helped me, you went through it all with me. I learned later how you had walked miles and miles through Shanghai all those afternoons when you were gone, searching for this very folk remedy. After I grew up, I understood you were not just trying to heal me but, more important, you were also teaching me to be strong in the face of my illness, my fear, and many, many difficulties in my long life later. You knew I would be all right once I learned that important lesson. And I was. Many years later, Nai Nai, I would have to be strong in the face of your own illness, and your death.

I remember my last visit to you. It was the summer of 1992. I had rushed to catch the first available plane from

Hawaii to Shanghai, and hurried from the airport to the critical ward in Jing An District Hospital. There was a heat wave, and the ward was packed with patients in their beds. Visiting family members were bumping into one another in the crowded room. The air, stirred by the slow ceiling fan, was sticky-warm and suffocating and smelled of sweat. I looked around and finally saw you, my ninety-seven-year-old Nai Nai. You lay quietly on a small corner bed with a bamboo-made mat on it, your face as pale as a sheet of rice paper, your 5'6" body shrunk so much it looked like a child's.

When I called you excitedly, you turned your head and looked at me. But there was no emotion, no recognition at all. I was confused. Why didn't you greet your dearest granddaughter, whom you had been thinking and talking about for months? Then Mom told me you had lost your memory and speech only the day before.

"I came home too late," I burst out, and tears streamed down my face. Something inside me collapsed. After all the suffering and struggling you had endured for nearly a century, so much of it for us . . . and now, when we had finally started to have a better life, you were leaving? No, I couldn't let you!

For two more weeks I watched you lie there, an oxygen tube in your nose, infusion needles in your purple-bloody legs and arms, suffering, struggling with death. Nai Nai, my heart was tearing apart! Every day, washing your small bony body made me cry. Nai Nai, you gave every drop of blood and every bit of energy to the people around you, day after day, year after year. Like a candle, you burned to the end to give light to others.

And finally, your light burned out.

You left us with great respect, not only from our family but also from lots of friends and neighbors. Nai Nai, did you hear my cry when you left? Did you see how I wouldn't let the staff take your body to the freezer box while it was still warm? I was afraid that you might wake up and find yourself alone in the dark in that cold metal box. So I waited there with you until your body grew cold and stiff.

Nai Nai, do you know the regrets I have had about you since your departure? I wish I had brought you to America to see what my life looks like, even for a short period of time; I wish I had said yes to many of your requests; I wish I had children, which you wanted so much, so you could be a great-grandmother to them. But the one thing I regret the most is that I never said to you, not even once, "I love you."

My American friends will be shocked to hear this. They will find it hard to understand this part of my culture—that despite the strong deep bond of love between us, we never expressed our deepest feelings verbally or with physical contact. We both knew of the love we shared. Our love was deeper than words, stronger than physical displays. Our love for each other filled our hearts.

Nai Nai, I know that I will dream of you many times again. And I know that no matter where I go in this world, you are with me always. For with true love comes the impossibility of true separation.

Now, I turn my head to the east, my eyes closed, facing my hometown thousands of miles away. And I whisper to you in the dark:

"Nai Nai, I love you."

AUTHOR'S NOTE

To write about my grandma was not a recent idea but an impulsive urge that came upon me ten years ago, a month after her passing.

I was watching the 1992 Olympics one night. Mark Lenzi had just won the gold medal in the three-meter springboard diving. He knelt down on the floor, hands covering his face for a moment, then said sadly, "This is for my grandmother. She was always very supportive of me. I wish she had seen this today. . . ." Tears were streaming down my face. Mark Lenzi's emotion released a flood of feelings in me for my grandma, of grief about her death, and of gratitude for her love. For I knew my grandma had done the same for me.

That night, I wrote a short piece about my grandma. I kept it in my drawer all these years.

Ten years have passed since she left us, but my memories of her and my feelings about her have not dimmed. Many times I felt the urge to share stories of her with others, our laughter and our tears, the good times and bad times we shared, and what she gave to this world as an ordinary woman. Who I am today has everything to do with her influence.

I am glad that you will now get to know her. And I hope that you will come to love her, just as I do.

JOAN ABELOVE

The Best Parts

Grandma Leah was renowned for her devotion to cleanliness. "Sleep, dear—I just want to change the sheets," she would whisper softly in your ear at 6 A.M., as she ripped the bottom sheet out from under you, yanked the top sheet off, and patted your head while pulling the pillowcase from under it.

Grandma Leah washed the linens every day, and she did it early because she was a busy woman. She had to do the laundry and scrub the gleaming white front steps of her Florida house before she went to work in my grandfather's store. It wasn't that she couldn't afford a cleaning lady—she could and did. But the house had to be "shipshape" so the cleaning lady didn't think Grandma Leah was a slob.

At Grandpa's men's clothing store, she kept the books and was the only female salesperson. She wore trifocals so that she could look up and read the writing on the shoeboxes on the very top shelves. I remember looking at her eyes and wondering how she could see anything through those lenses with the two thick lines dividing them into three parts.

Behind the lenses, her eyes looked like a Picasso painting.

She was proud of "The Store," as my grandfather called it. Its actual name was The Peerless, and that was what Grandma Leah always called it: The Peerless—I think because she felt it was truly without peers. That was certainly the way she felt about herself. When she took me shopping for clothes, she would glance at the first rack of dresses in the girls' department, run one hand across them, lift her nose in the air as she turned to the salesgirl, and say haughtily, "I'd like to see some of your *better* things."

When Grandma Leah was in her seventies and I was a teenager, my grandfather bought her a dishwasher. My parents said that he did it to drive her crazy, since my grandmother did not believe that any machine could clean as well as she could. She washed the dishes before she put them in the dishwasher, and then she washed them again after she took them out. The machine might have sullied her clean dishes.

Every December, my parents and I took an overnight train to spend a week in Florida with these grandparents. We would board the train in New York City in the afternoon and find our compartment. During the day, the roomette was just two rows of seats facing each other with a tiny bathroom, so small only one person could squeeze inside at a time. We would sit in our little room until it was time for dinner.

I loved eating dinner in the dining car. The table jiggled and the glasses and plates slid around on the table. The silverware was big and very heavy. Water sloshed around in the water glasses, sometimes splashing onto the bright white tablecloth. Coffee and tea were served in shiny, silvery, heavy urns. After the waiter poured the coffee and tea, coffee from my father's coffee cup and tea from my mother's sloshed into their saucers. The food didn't dance around on our plates, but it was quite a feat to spear the piece of food you wanted. You aimed your fork at a French fry but it was never in the same place when the fork reached the plate.

We ate watching Baltimore go by. "Look," my mother said, "all the houses are connected." Small apartment buildings sat right next to one another. It all looked very cozy to me, an only child who always wanted other kids to be in closer proximity.

When we went back to our compartment, it had been transformed. The porter had come in and made up the berths—a lower and upper bunk bed—for us to sleep in. The compartment had become much smaller, with only enough room for two people to stand at a time. One person had to be in a berth or in the bathroom if the other two were going to stand up. Cozy. I loved it. I would flop down on the lower berth and raise the shade. There I was all snuggled in bed, looking out as the world went by. My parents would sleep in the upper berth so I could stay in the lower one and look out the window.

When it was time to go to sleep, I looked out and saw Washington, D.C., the dome of the Capitol shining. One trip I woke up suddenly when the train stopped in the middle of the night. I raised the shade and there I was, lying in bed in my pajamas looking out at a train station in what I was sure was a small town in Georgia. I didn't see any passengers in the station. It was dark beyond the dim lights on the platform, but I imagined people asleep in houses off in the distance, people who, if they woke up and looked out their windows, could see me, looking through the train window. Every trip after that, I would try and make sure I woke myself up in the middle of the night so I could see this train station in Georgia again.

I was supposed to have been born in Georgia. My father was stationed on an army base there when my mother was pregnant with me. When my mother was in her ninth month, her obstetrician flew to Detroit to attend his brother's funeral and was killed when his plane crashed. With no other obstetrician on the base, my mother took a bus to Florida, where her mother lived, to have me. My father told me that when he joined her there two weeks later, my mother was "a nervous wreck." My father blamed Grandma Leah and told her to stop driving her daughter crazy. Grandma Leah was outraged. No one told her how to behave. She took to bed and stayed there. Even when my mother came home from the hospital, Grandma Leah stayed in bed and never saw me, her first and only grandchild, until she came to visit us when I was almost a year old.

In the morning, when the conductor announced "Bradenton!" the train stop just before ours, my mother would say, "Time to get dressed." My mother called Bradenton my dressing room. For the next half hour my mother dressed me in my best dress, socks and shoes, brushed me off, and put a bow in my hair. (These were the only times in my life that I ever wore a bow in my very short hair.) She would get me all ready and then I would have to stand until the train arrived in Sarasota, so I wouldn't get, God forbid, wrinkled.

When the conductor yelled "Sarasota!" we would go stand in the doorway. I loved that first blast of Florida air—the sweet, clinging dampness of it, the muggy smell that still means those winter Florida visits to me—and the ridiculous sight of palm trees decorated with Christmas lights. As we pulled into the station, there were tall dark-green hibiscus bushes spotted with bright red flowers, and in front of them, clusters of old people looking up at the train windows for their grandchildren. That's why we were in the door, so my grandmother could see us clearly and first. And then she would see us. Her arms would open wide, her knees would bend the tiniest bit, she would beam and hug me in her hard, unyielding body hug. Maybe some of the hardness of her hugs was the fault of the corset she always wore, a long contraption that started under her breasts, ended at her hips, and laced tightly up her front. My grandfather would stand just off to the side of her, ignored, but smiling at me.

Staying in Grandma's house was like visiting a foreign country—things looked the same, but the rules were all different. Grandma Leah did not believe in wastepaper baskets and did not have a single one anywhere in the house. If you wanted to throw something away, you had to walk through the house into the attached garage, where there was a small wastepaper basket to the left of the door. Food and drink were not allowed anywhere in the house except in the kitchen—or in the dining room if Grandma had set the table there. Ants. The big danger was attracting ants. I thought that no ant in its right mind would dare enter my grandmother's house, no matter what wonderful thing it smelled.

But I never brought even a glass of water out of the kitchen. Grandma Leah had her rules, and no one ever broke them. If you didn't finish every morsel on your plate, she would say, "But you left the best part!" and you would have to eat that last lima bean. We obeyed her rules, but no one took her very seriously. We all made fun of her bizarre ways. We would say, "Sleep, dear," or "But you left the best part!" pointing to a chicken bone. My father's big joke was that Grandma Leah had wanted my mother to marry him solely because he was in the laundry business and she thought cleanliness was next to godliness. Sometimes Grandma would smile when he said this; mostly she would ignore him.

I insisted on bringing a set of about twenty Barbie-size dolls every trip. One of my other grandmother's friends had crocheted beautiful clothes for each doll. They sat on my dresser at home, and I knew they were the only things of mine that would be allowed to be displayed in Grandma's den, the room I slept in. I loved the dolls. I loved their bright, cheery outfits, each one entirely different from all the others. And they helped make the room feel a little bit mine.

Maybe because my dolls took up so much space or maybe for some other reason, my mother never brought any books to read to me. But early on, she discovered that among the well-dusted, never-opened, color-coordinated, leather-bound books on Grandma's living room shelves was a copy of *Just So Stories* by Rudyard Kipling. My bedtime ritual at Grandma's always included my mother reading to me and then our reciting together, "Them that takes cakes which the Parsee-man bakes, makes dreadful mistakes," and my favorite, "I am the cat who walks by himself, and all places are alike to me."

Our days were pretty free, except for the one day my grandmother would take me clothes shopping, to buy me some better things. Other than that, my mother and father and I would go swimming in the Gulf of Mexico. The beach had a pool right next to it, and my father taught me how to dive in that pool. Other days, they would take me to the driving range where my father taught me how to hit golf balls, or to a tennis court where I took lessons from the tennis pro, or to a stable where I took horseback-riding lessons. My grandmother never came with us on these excursions. She was always at work in the store.

"I love you more than life itself," Grandma Leah would say to me. "More than life itself." She said this all the time. It made sense to me. She probably did love me more than life, but not more than clothes, cleaning, and order. Life was not one of Grandma's priorities. Once she said, "I love you more than your other grandmother," and hugged me in her stiff, unbending body hug. I knew it wasn't true—I knew Grandma Sophie adored me—but I also knew why Grandma Leah would make that claim. She did buy me more clothes and more presents than my father's mother. No matter that she bought me what *she* wanted me to have, not what I wanted. She spent more money, and that was the yardstick she used for love. Never mind that I stayed with Grandma Sophie every weekend, that she told me stories about my father and his two sisters when they were little, let me drink 7UP straight from the bottle in the living room, let me play pretend games with all of her china figurines, made me fried matzo for breakfast, taught me how to play poker, and helped me drag her satin quilt off her bed and down to the living room where I could snuggle up with it on the floor and watch Sid Caesar on TV every Saturday night. Grandma Sophie's gifts cost nothing. She never took me clothes shopping or bought me hard, expensive, unhuggable stuffed animals.

One afternoon each visit, my mother took me to the cemetery to visit her brother Irving's grave. I loved these trips. She referred to him, and so did I, as Uncle Irving, although he died before I was born. He was her younger brother, her only sibling, and she adored him. He died when he was twenty-one, just married, and living in my parents' house while they were in Georgia. My mother never went back to that house. She had it sold before they returned. The last time she had seen Irving was in the train station when she and my father were leaving for the army. She always cried when we went to that train station.

On the way to visit his grave, we would stop and buy two bouquets of gladiolas. One was for Uncle Irving, the other we divided between my great-grandfather and great-grand-mother. That was the first thing we did, divide the gladiolas.

Then we wandered around the cemetery. There was never another living soul there. The ground was sandy, and burrs clung to my socks. My mother would go back and sit and cry by Uncle Irving's grave. I would go to see the one gravestone that had a picture on it, an old faded picture covered by a plastic bubble to protect it. It was a smiling young woman with an old-fashioned hairdo and old-fashioned clothes. I liked her. I wondered if she had wanted her picture on the stone. I wondered if she could see it now, smile at it herself. I was glad there was someone there who seemed as if she had been alive, like my Uncle Irving.

My mother told me so many stories about Uncle Irving, I felt like I had known him. She had a picture of him on her desk at home, a picture of him standing proudly next to a gigantic swordfish he had caught. Irving was six feet tall and so was the fish. In her top desk drawer, my mother kept one of the fish's scales.

My mother would finish crying, and I would wander back to sit next to her. She told me stories about what a great sense of humor Uncle Irving had, how sweet he was, how handsome he was, how much he would have loved me. Then she picked the burrs off my socks, hugged me, and we'd drive back. No one else ever came with us on these excursions.

Grandma kept a picture of Uncle Irving in her living room in a gleaming silver frame. Every day she floated fresh gardenias in a silver bowl next to his picture. The only thing I ever heard her say about Uncle Irving was that he was very handsome and a wonderful dresser.

Grandma kept a picture of me on another table in her

living room, also in a thick, silver frame. Every year, my parents sent her my school picture for that frame. One year, I was dressed in a striped T-shirt and denim overalls. My hair was tousled, and I looked like I was having the time of my life. My grandmother refused to put that picture in her silver frame. The one from the previous year stayed there until the next school picture arrived a year later. Pants should never be worn by girls and certainly not displayed in a silver frame.

One evening every trip, we went out to a fancy restaurant on Lido Beach. That night, my grandmother would get really dressed up—very high-heeled shoes, of which she had about fifty pairs hung in shoe bags on the back of her closet doors. Grandma had four closets full of clothes, all hung neatly in plastic bags that didn't touch one another. When she got dressed up, she would put on a ring with an enormous purple amethyst stone. The stone was so big it looked like it could pick up Martian radio frequencies.

At the restaurant, we all listened to the waiter recite the specials of the day. I always ordered pompano. I didn't know until years later that pompano was fish. Ordinarily, I hated fish and refused to eat it, but the waiter had once recommended pompano and it had sounded exotic, and it was delicious.

After Grandma Leah had asked how each entrée was prepared and when she had decided what she wanted, she closed her menu, placed it on top of her plate, and went to the bathroom to wash her hands. She returned with her elbows tight against her waist, her forearms at a 90-degree angle with her body, her hands dangling limply from her wrists. She held her hands this way, not touching anything, until the first course arrived. Only then would she pick up whatever utensil was needed to eat the appetizer. After her hands had been sullied by the fork or spoon, she then returned them to the napkin on her lap, between courses. I always wondered if she worried that the silverware was clean enough, or that the napkins might be dirty. All she could be sure of was her own hands, which she had personally washed and kept away from anything but air. If she had eaten with her hands, it might have made sense for her to take such care of them. But, of course, she didn't.

When I was nine, we arrived in Florida as usual and went to a play that evening. During the play, I started to feel sick. By the time we got back to Grandma's, I had a fever. The next morning, I felt worse. My throat was so sore I couldn't swallow anything, not even my own saliva. My mother got me a towel and I lay in bed, drooling into the towel. She got the name of a pediatrician from one of Grandma's friends. "I'm sure he'll be nice," she told me. "With a name like that he has to be." His name was Dr. Butcher.

He came and examined me. Years later, my mother told me that Dr. Butcher had said that I was faking, that I was getting up in the middle of the night and eating and that I was feigning this illness to gain attention.

From the moment I got sick, my grandmother absented herself. Once a day she would stand in the doorway outside my room and peer in, expressionless as usual. My bed was on the other side of the room. She came no closer to me than that. My mother sat by my bed, read to me, changed my towel, sponged me down when my fever spiked. But my grandmother never came within touching distance. My other relatives came every day, my two aunts, my uncle, my cousin. They brought me treats that they knew I loved, trying to get me to eat. My cousin Robert brought me a "banana blizzard," my favorite ice-cream treat in the world, only available in Florida. He was sure that would get me to eat. When I couldn't, he looked worried. He tried again, and I rolled over. I couldn't look at his face. It made me nervous.

Dr. Butcher came every day, examined me, and left. I thought it was strange that he didn't give me any medicine. I thought it was strange that I was not getting better, that for a week, all I could do was lie in bed and drool into a towel. After a week, my parents thought so, too, and placed a long-distance phone call to my pediatrician back home, who told them to get me to a hospital immediately, that what I had was a serious infection that was making a lot of kids sick back home.

Grandma never came to the hospital. At the time, I didn't think much about it. Once I was in the hospital, there were the nicest nurses' aides who brought me comic books and Coke, when I could swallow, and made jokes about the steaks and French fries they were feeding me through the I.V. I was hooked up to. I was having a good time and wasn't thinking about the fact that my grandmother, who said she loved me more than life itself, had not come near me since I had gotten sick.

When I was well enough to leave the hospital and my mother had me set up in my room at Grandma's, Grandma Leah appeared in the doorway. My mother was adjusting the blinds, so that the sunlight didn't stream in on me. As she lowered a blind, it banged gently against the wall. "Oh," Grandma Leah gasped. Just "Oh."

My mother dropped the blind pull and whirled around. "So this is what matters to you?" my mother screamed. "Your wall! The paint on your wall! The slightest chip in the paint on your wall!"

My grandmother stood in the doorway, expressionless and silent.

My mother shrieked, "You've already buried a son! Do you want to bury a daughter, too?"

Then all was silence. My grandmother stood there for another second, turned, and left. My mother finished adjusting the blinds, came over and adjusted my pillows, and left, too.

I was too stunned to say a word. My mother never raised her voice and she *never* did anything in violation of my grandmother's rules. My mother wrote a letter to her mother every day of her life, at least a one-page letter, never a postcard. When my grandparents used to visit us, my grandmother would send her trunk up a week before her arrival. My mother would unpack her mother's clothes, iron them, and hang them up in the guest room closet, ready for

Grandma's arrival. My mother spent a year remodeling our house when I was five. She pored over architectural drawings, paint chips, shower doors, bathroom tiles, wallpaper possibilities. When the house was done, my mother had what was called "a nervous breakdown." She went to bed and stayed there for a few weeks. I was furious that she had deserted me. I took a crayon and drew all over a patch of the new wallpaper in the hall outside her closed door. Much later, I learned that her breakdown happened just as Grandma Leah was scheduled to visit, to inspect the house my mother had designed.

Grandma Leah didn't enter my room until I was well enough to be out of bed. Years later, when my mother was in the hospital with a malignant brain tumor, Grandma Leah did not come to see her. And when my mother died, Grandma Leah did not come to the funeral. My grandfather, she told us, was too ill to travel, and she could not leave him. I wasn't surprised. That was what Grandma Leah was like.

I never thought about it. I never questioned anything about Grandma Leah. She had always been odd, but I never thought about why. What had she been so afraid of, or so angry about, that she became such a shell of a person? It wasn't until much later that an aunt on my father's side told me how shocked she had been at Grandma Leah's behavior. "When her only daughter was sick, she didn't come. When she was dying, she didn't come. And when she died, she didn't come."

It was only recently that I started really thinking about

Grandma Leah. Had she been the way I knew her all her life, or had it been a reaction to losing her son? And did my mother's words to her about burying her daughter reverberate in her brain, make it impossible to visit that daughter when she was dying and to bury her when she died? Was this the only way she could deal with outliving first one and then both of her children?

I will never know what made Grandma Leah tick. But I think of her often. I think about how strongly Grandma Leah affected my mother, and how little I always felt she had affected me, how I dismissed her as not being an important figure in my life. But now I recognize Grandma Leah in me—when I am outraged that my son does not pick up his socks even after I have asked him to, when my husband pours himself some orange juice and leaves a small splotch on the kitchen counter, when my best friend arrives a few minutes late after she promised to be on time. Name a messy part of life, and I feel Grandma Leah's antiseptic spirit rising angrily from deep inside of me.

And then I think about my son, when he was four months old, spending a half hour studying every millimeter of a rubber hamburger toy for dogs, as if it were the Rosetta stone. I think about how wonderful it felt to watch him, to not interrupt or distract him, to not hand him another toy that might have been more educational, more age-appropriate, cleaner, more appealing to me.

At these times, I take a deep breath—slowly in, slowly out—decide again that genes are not destiny, and think how much more fun Grandma Leah would have had if she had enjoyed me as well as loved me, if she had laughed along with Grandpa, if she had feasted on the whole wonderful, messy, sad, and joyous world instead of leaving the best parts.

AUTHOR'S NOTE

When I was asked to submit a short story about how my grandmother influenced my life, I immediately thought I would write about Grandma Sophie. As a child, I stayed at her house on weekends and loved it. She was fun and warm and full of life. She told me lots of funny stories about my father and his two sisters and about her own history. She came over from Russia with her father as a young woman, got a factory job on the Lower East Side, became active in the workers' rights movement, became a Socialist, and was hit over the head by one of her bosses who was enraged by her demand that toilet paper be available in the bathrooms. So I began writing about her.

But the back of my brain kept thinking about my other grandmother, Grandma Leah, the one who was not warm, who was not fun, who—as far as I knew—had led an exceedingly uneventful, boring life. And I kept thinking about her. So one day, I sat down and made a list of what I could write about Grandma Leah—and I remembered a lot of funny stories, many of which I've included in "The Best Parts." But how had she influenced my life? It was only when

I kept writing, and began to remember how much she had affected my own mother, that it became clear to me that it was Grandma Leah I wanted to write about, because she had affected my life in ways I never realized.

ALMA FLOR ADA

My Abuelita, My Paradise

*To Camilita: I love you as much
as she loved me.*

I wake up to a familiar fragrance. The heavy perfume of jasmine and gardenia still lingers in the morning air, yet it is the scent of talcum powder on my grandmother's skin that tells me it is time to begin a new day.

I am already in her arms. Dressed all in white, her starched cotton dress fresh and cool to the touch in the already-warm morning, Abuelita walks lightly out of the house and onto the wide porch.

I am not fully ready to wake up yet, and keep opening my eyes and then closing them again. Her steps quicken. We are under the flame trees now. As I open my eyes, I see the sky covered by the startling flowers. My eyes remain open, filled with this explosion of red and orange blossoms.

Abuelita's steps are longer, purposeful; we are almost at our destination. When we reach the pastures, I hear her voice for the first time this morning, as she greets the cow-hands. It is a deep, kind voice. Each word is articulated clearly and precisely, as neat as her own handwriting on the chalkboard. Always wanting to be understood, always making it easier for others to follow her thoughts.

As a teacher of children and adults; as the mother of a large household; as she taught me to read, playfully drawing the names of plants and flowers on the earth with a stick, my grandmother was always clear, direct, patient. Her life was constant teaching. I lost her when I was barely six years old, yet she taught me more than anyone else in my entire life.

The men in the meadow respond joyfully to her greeting. Her presence awakens a positive response in people, even in those who do not know her. Is it on account of the openness in her large eyes, as she looks frankly into theirs? Maybe it is the firmness of her stance, which seems to say, *I know I'm here, and I know I'm a good person. I see you, and I trust that you, too, are a good person.* Or is it the smile that seems to linger on her mouth, like a tiny seedling ready to sprout into laughter?

I do not question the reasons why; I am used to this response, not only because it is my own, but also because I see it all around me. I see it in my parents, in my aunts and uncles, in the people who work on the farm, in those who come knocking at the door, and in those who pass by on the road in the afternoons, while she and I sit on the large porch, waiting for the sunset.

One of the cowhands approaches, leading a cow with her calf. While the mother nuzzles her calf, he begins to milk her, right there in the meadow, squatting on the grass. The milk begins to fall into the large bucket and then my grandmother hands him the shiny aluminum jug she has brought with us. It is soon filled to the brim with warm milk.

My grandmother lets me drink first. She knows I delight

in the light foam that soon leaves me with a white mustache and beard. I breathe deeply, inhaling the morning air filled with the smell of grass, cows, manure, and fresh milk. I am now ready for the new day, and my grandmother sets me on the ground.

I have to walk fast to keep up with her on our return home. She slows down for me a little but keeps up a brisk pace. I know she needs to catch a bus to take her to work. She is a school principal; her school will soon be full of teachers and children and she wants to make sure she arrives before anyone else, to greet them all with her kind words and her reassuring smile.

Her name was Dolores Salvador Méndez, but most people called her Lola or, endearingly, Lolita. Having been born at a difficult time, during Cuba's War of Independence, my grandmother was not able to attend school as a child. Her own mother had never gone to school, had never learned to read and write. When Lola was already in her late teens, her father, who had become wealthy after the war, sent her and her younger sisters to a private boarding school in Havana, the capital of the country. Lola suffered great shame and humiliation for her lack of previous schooling, but she made an extraordinary effort and graduated first in her class. She also became determined to teach others—and to do it with kindness and love, making learning meaningful and exciting, unlike the traditional methods prevalent in those times.

We enter the house through the back door. She rinses out the milk jug and then fills a drinking glass with water. The water drips from the filtering stone into a clay receptacle that keeps it cool and fresh. Grandmother savors every drop. When the glass is empty, she says to me, "Water is such a miracle! Such a gift!" And her words leave me with a sense of wonder for the rest of the day.

She has taught me to see miracles everywhere, in the tiny round leaves of the myrtle hedge, in the delicious sweetness of a mango or the tartness of a tamarind. We walk through the orchard, picking fruit from the trees, receiving each one as a personal gift. She always reminds me how that fruit began as a little seed, a seed with a will to grow—how, aided by soil and water and sun, the seed turned into a tree, which now generously gives us ripe fruit, offering us joy.

Filled with this awareness, I live in constant wonder. Even though she is away at her school for many hours, I feel her by my side as I watch the constant toil of ants carrying leaves ten times their size to their anthill. I feel her standing with me under the orange trees, as I breathe in the perfume of the fragrant blossoms. She is with me as I hunt for lizards' eggs, gathering them and placing them in the soft mossy hollows beneath the ferns, a perfect spot for little lizards to hatch and emerge into the world.

When she returns from her school, tired and hot, she heads straight for the shower. Only then, dressed in a light housedress, will she sit down for lunch. Everyone else who lives with us—my parents, aunts, and uncles—has already eaten, being on a different schedule. So I have her all to myself again.

She always has something to tell me. Often the events of the day remind her of previous experiences, of something that happened once upon a time to a family member. Other times, she is reminded of a Greek myth, a fairy tale, or a fable. And so reality and fantasy are interwoven as she introduces me to a world that extends far beyond the limits of our small town.

Her passion for learning was unending. Having arrived late to books and formal schooling, she seemed to never get her fill of new knowledge. Besides Spanish, her native language, she learned to speak English and French. And she enjoyed reading literature, particularly poetry, in all three languages. Every topic interested her, but she had a particular love for Cuban history and for classical Greek mythology, both of which she made real and familiar to me. When I wondered about the taste of "nectar and ambrosia," the food of the gods and goddesses on Mount Olympus, she answered matter-of-factly that they tasted like *nísperos*, the delicate fruit growing in our yard. From that time on, I always expected to see a goddess or two walking in our garden, ready to pick some *nísperos*.

After lunch is the perfect time of day for some quiet. Abuelita carries her hammock on her shoulder and holds my hand. Again we walk out of the house, along the long avenue of flame trees, this time down to the river. We cross the shallows, stepping on stones so that our shoes will not get wet, and climb onto the island. The *Tínima* is an old river, and its meanderings have created inlets. This particular inlet is the largest, so it deserves the name of island. It is covered with many coconut trees, and a few cashews and guavas. At the center stands a majestic caimito tree, a benign protective giant.

Abuelita decides to hang her hammock in the bamboo grove. There, under the rustling bamboo leaves that sound like distant ocean waves, she sleeps her siesta.

I love to see her sleep. She becomes one with the whole earth, the earth that feels so firm beneath my feet, that invites me to wander around the trees. An earth always generous with her gifts: a beautiful tree snail shell, bright yellow with black edges; extraordinary seeds, smooth and shiny *peonías*, with little red-and-black faces; wonderful maroon *mates*, strong and rough. I add them to my collection of treasures, the precious pebbles already in my apron pocket.

When Abuelita wakes up, it is time for me to take a bath, to get dressed up in a clean starched dress, and to have my hair combed in two braids with large bows at the ends. Then I am ready to go on my evening search for *maravilla* flowers, multicolor trumpets that stay closed during the heat of the day, opening only in the late afternoon.

Abuelita receives my flowers, strung on blades of grass, and ties them into small garlands. In a familiar ritual, we will place the garlands on top of her piano, between the bust of José Martí, one of our revered patriots, whose story she has often told, and a doll that someone brought Abuelita from Guatemala. The doll represents the Guatemalan girl who loved the poet Martí, and who died of a broken heart.

For Abuelita, reading was not only an intellectual curiosity. The ideas from her readings inspired her life. She believed in women's creativity, strength, and rights. She rode horses and convinced my grandfather to buy one of the first automobiles to circulate in Cuba. She was the first woman in our town to cut her hair short and to hem her skirts high above her ankles. Some people criticized her because she allowed her daughters to go out without stockings and to wear pants. And some got very angry at her when she began knocking at the doors of wealthy houses, inviting the maids who answered to attend the night school she had opened for working women. "If you study, you will not have to spend your life cleaning someone else's house," she told them. Initially, the women were afraid, not believing that they truly could break away from the bondage they had inherited from their mothers and grand-mothers, some of whom had worked as slaves. But finally they filled her classroom. Whenever anyone showed great interest, Abuelita would invite her to also attend her day school, and found ways to help her do so. People protested that grown women should not be sitting in school with their children, but Abuelita prevailed. Many of these women later became teachers.

Once the garlands are delivered, we watch the sunset, counting the bats that begin flying out of their nests under the roof of our porch. Abuelita's stories follow one after another, like the *maravilla* flowers I have strung on blades of grass, forming an unending garland.

One special Saturday, Abuelita is full of excitement. The bee man is here. Instead of going out to the pastures for milk, we drink a cold glass of milk from the fridge. There is no time to waste. Out in the fields, by the elm grove, stands a large old tree with a hollow trunk. The bees have had their beehive there for years, since my mother was a little girl, and perhaps even before. Once a year, the bee man gathers the fruit of their labor, the wonderful honeycomb. He lights some grass and uses the dark smoke to drive the bees out of the hive. Undaunted by the hundreds of bees flying around, he dips his arms into the hive and brings out the honeycomb, piece by piece. He fills several buckets and delivers them to the kitchen. My grandmother is ready for them. She will keep some of the honeycomb in tightly sealed jars to use during the course of the year. The rest she squeezes dry, setting aside the fine white wax. The dark honey goes into her large round-bellied copper pot. She lights a bright coal fire in the old tiled stove. As the honey begins to bubble, she stirs it constantly with a long-handle wooden spoon.

Drops of sweat cover her skin, and she frequently wipes her forehead with a large white kerchief. Red from the fire, her beloved face looks prettier to me than ever. My gaze moves from the glow on her face to the honey in the pot, slowly turning into taffy.

Every so often, she lets a drop of taffy fall into a cup of water, to test the thickness of the golden mass. It takes a very long time for the taffy to be ready, but I could stay forever in the hot kitchen, drowsy from the smell of honey, watching my grandmother's arm stir, stir, stir, and the smile on her face spreading until it is brighter than the coal fire, than the copper pot.

The taffy is finally ready, and we begin the long process of kneading it. We cover our hands with butter to work the hot taffy, and we pull and blend, and pull again. After a while, our hands are red and burning, but the taffy is changing color, from a deep, dark gold to a soft, light golden shine. We break off pieces to place on wax paper on the massive kitchen table. Every so often, we each place one on our tongues instead. The taffy dissolves slowly in our mouths, the love in our hearts expanding like the taffy, filling our hearts like the smell of honey fills the kitchen.

Abuelita's last dream was to create a nursery school for children of working mothers. There was no such institution in Cuba, but she had read that it existed in France, where it was called a crèche. She did not have the money to create such a project, but she had the farm that she had inherited from her father. She donated some land that ran along the length of the farm so that a road could be built on it. In turn, she obtained a promise from the town authorities that they would build the crèche.

That year, on the tenth of October, the day that Cubans celebrate the War of Independence and the abolition of slavery, Abuelita held a major celebration in front of our house. A cornerstone was placed for the building that would hold the crèche, and Abuelita gave a passionate speech. She told the townspeople that the land had been donated to build an avenue, and that she wanted the avenue to be named after the patriot Amalia Simoni, a woman who had supported the independence movement and who had been born in the same house that later became our family home. Abuelita spoke about the right of women to have paid work, the right of children to be well cared for while their mothers worked, the right of everyone to receive an education.

Next morning, my mother and I, puzzled at not seeing Abuelita up and about, went to her room. She looked surprisingly still. The mosquito netting around her bed moved softly in the morning breeze, and gave the illusion that she was still breathing. But she had died in her sleep. Without her presence and encouragement, it took a long time for that crèche to be built. But to this day, her students still speak admiringly about how much they learned from her, and many women are still grateful to her for helping them change their lives.

Some years ago, while I was in Cuba visiting my hometown of Camagüey, I happened to run into one of these women, who was by then a school principal. Recognizing me, she insisted that I accompany her to her house. There in her living room hung a photo of my grandmother, and under it, honoring her memory, was a vase filled with fresh flowers.

I used to call her *Mi Paraíso*, My Paradise. Her memory is still my secret paradise, the place I return to, again and again, for nourishment and inspiration.

AUTHOR'S NOTE

It has always been difficult for me to write about my own family, because we each have our own memories of the events we shared, and I feel a great respect for each person's unique experiences.

My grandmother was many things to many people. She was a daughter to my great-grandmother, who lived in a small house next to ours; sister to several sisters and one brother; aunt and great-aunt; mother of five; grandmother of three at the time of her death, and grandmother to many more who were born afterward. She was a source of inspiration and a beloved wife to her poet husband, who always treated her as such, and a model for many women who admired her as a public speaker and a writer. Yet perhaps it was as a teacher that she influenced the most people.

My memories of her are, of course, only my own. I knew her for just a few years, and only as a child. Others knew her much longer, and as adults. If others were to describe her, they probably would emphasize different qualities. I'm delighted by this opportunity to share what she meant to me. Writing this text from my own perspective has helped me to realize yet again the power of words, especially the written word. By honoring our own reality, we re-create ourselves; by preserving our memories, we rediscover the significance of our present. Nothing would please me more than to know that by sharing the memories I have of my grandmother and the meaning she holds in my life, I have inspired my readers to remember someone significant in their own lives, to treasure their own memories, and perhaps even to share and preserve those memories in writing.

BIOGRAPHIES

JOAN ABELOVE lives in New York City with her husband, their son, and two cats. She works full-time as a technical writer in downtown Manhattan and writes fiction whenever she can. So far, she has written two young adult novels (*Go and Come Back* and *Saying It Out Loud*), and is in the process of writing her third.

According to **ALMA FLOR ADA**, "Words, imagery, and the poetry they create have been a perennial source of joy for me. They have given wings to my fantasy and roots to my spirit. In a life lived in many different parts of the world, they have been the only constant home. Throughout it all, childhood memories and books—the nurturing and life examples of the former and the intellectual stimulation of the latter— have created the environment to sustain a family, to continue to grow."

Alma Flor Ada was blessed to be born into a family where words and stories were essential. Her maternal grandfather, Medardo Lafuente, was a poet and a journalist. Her paternal grandfather, Modesto Ada Barral, directed a newspaper and a radio station. Her grandmother, Lola Salvador, made the world of history and mythology come alive through storytelling. And her father wove the evolution of humankind and civilizations into an unending tale, sharing one chapter each night at bedtime.

Today, Alma Flor Ada is an internationally published children's book author whose many works include poetry, picture books, autobiographies, retellings of folktales, plays, songs, and translations. She has received many awards for her work, including the Pura Belpré Award, the Christopher Award, the José Martí World Award, and the Museum of

Tolerance Award. *The School Library Journal* called her picture book *Gathering the Sun* "an important book." She is currently the director of the Center for Multicultural Education at the University of San Fransisco. Her most recent book is *Pio Peep*, a bilingual collection of Hispanic nursery rhymes. You can visit her online at www.almaflorada.com.

Born in Saranac Lake, New York, in 1951, **BONNIE CHRISTENSEN** attended nine schools between grades K and 12 and was generally referred to as "the new kid." After graduating from the University of Vermont, she moved to New York City, where she worked in Off Broadway theater, primarily at Joseph Papp's New York Shakespeare Festival and then at the Screen Actors Guild. After thirteen years in New York, she longed to wiggle her toes in the spring mud and returned to Vermont. Back in Vermont she married, had a daughter, and became a book illustrator and writer. Bonnie has illustrated two books for adults and seven books for children, including three she also wrote. She and her daughter, Emily, spend a few months each year living and working in Italy. You can visit her online at www.bonniechristensen.com.

BEVERLY CLEARY is one of America's most popular authors of children's fiction. Born in McMinnville, Oregon, she lived on a farm in Yamhill until she was six and moved to Portland. After college, she became the children's librarian in Yakima, Washington. In 1940, she married Clarence T. Cleary, and they are the parents of twins.

Mrs. Cleary's books have earned her many prestigious awards, including the American Library Association's Laura Ingalls Wilder Award, presented in recognition of her lasting contribution to children's literature. Her *Dear Mr. Henshaw* was awarded the 1984 John Newbery Medal, and her *Ramona and Her Father* and *Ramona Quimby, Age 8* have been named

Newbery Honor books. In addition, her books have won more than twenty-five statewide awards based on the votes of her young readers. Her characters—such as Henry Huggins, Ellen Tebbits, Otis Spofford, and Beezus and Ramona Quimby, as well as Ribsy, Socks, and Ralph S. Mouse—have delighted children for more than two generations. You can visit her online at www.beverlycleary.com.

In addition to the Coretta Scott King, the Orbis Pictus, and the *Boston Globe–Horn Book* awards, **PAT CUMMINGS** has been the recipient of 9 T-shirts, 13 mugs, 315 ballerina drawings, and 1 embroidered pillow from readers. She has been illustrating children's books ever since her graduation from Pratt Institute in the mid-1970s. Ten years later, she began writing them as well when she realized that exposing her younger brother's childhood exploits was an ideal means of revenge. Repeatedly changing Artie's name (to avoid legal action) has made it possible for her to sneak several books about him into print.

Currently, Pat and her husband, Chuku Lee, live in a loft in beautiful downtown Brooklyn, New York. Their cat, Cash, occasionally models for her books, as do family members and friends both willingly and unwittingly.

Ms. Cummings recalls, "My father was in the army, and, as a result, we were constantly traveling. We never lived anywhere for more than three years at a time. My sisters and brother and I were always 'the new kids on the block.'" She appreciates having been exposed to different places and lifestyles and still likes to travel and learn about other cultures. Now it is research for different books that leads her to African marketplaces, castles in Spain, or unexplored corners of New York City.

Through the years, drawing was a constant form of entertainment and a handy ice-breaker in new school situations. "In fifth grade, I did a healthy business selling ballerina drawings during recess. My dancers had pinpoint waists, huge flowered tutus, and legs that tapered down to tiny, needle-like toe shoes . . . Luckily, my parents encouraged my interest in art. My whole family was and is a very close-knit and supportive unit.

"I grew up in the fairy-tale generation. My earliest memories are of stories that my mother read to us from a book called *Tales of the Rhine*. We lived in Germany then and would visit castles along the Rhine that made the stories come to life. I recall scenes with dragons and princesses and heroes who turned into stars. The book really had few illustrations, but I still remember scenes as they appeared in my mind while she read."

Ms. Cummings does not recall having many picture books with positive Black characters as a child. Her goal now is to ensure that children who read her books will "find a bit of themselves, their world and their stories" reflected in the pages. "I want the book to be worth the time children spend with it . . . so they have to find something between the pages that strengthens them, informs them, embraces or just tickles them. Then, the book works."

Born in Washington, D.C., in 1919, and raised in a family of naturalists, **JEAN CRAIGHEAD GEORGE** has centered her life around nature and writing. She attended Pennsylvania State University, graduating with degrees in English and science. During the 1940s she was a member of the White House press corps and a reporter for *The Washington Post*. Ms. George has written more than 90 books, among them *My Side of the Mountain*, a Newbery Honor Book, plus two sequels, and the 1973 Newbery Medal winner, *Julie of the Wolves*, which was also followed by two sequels.

Ms. George has won more than twenty national and international awards for her young-adult work. She branched into picture books when her granddaughters, Rebecca and Caity, were born. Upon the arrival of her grandsons, she joined artist Wendell Minor in a series of nature-adventure books for boys. These are set on the tundra, in the mountains, and on the wild rivers of America.

When writing her books, Ms. George camps in the environment she is writing about, interviews scientists, and, when possible, raises the animal protagonists. Over the years she has raised at least 173 different animals, including raccoons, minks, foxes, crows, robins, frogs, lizards, and many others. She has not raised wolves, but a wolf friend, Koda, welcomes her to the home of Doug and Lynne Sues, Koda's alphas, with licks and soft whimpers.

In addition to writing books, Ms. George is now working with composer Chris Kubie to bring music into her children's books in this, the age of acoustics. You can visit her online at www.jeancraigheadgeorge.com.

Born of Chinese parents in Myanmar, **MINFONG HO** grew up in an airy wooden house on the outskirts of Bangkok, Thailand, where her bedroom window overlooked rice fields and water buffaloes. Her first language was Cantonese, which she spoke with her family, including her grandmother. She later absorbed Thai from the markets and street life, and then learned English in school.

It was while she was a homesick student at Cornell University, in upstate New York, that Minfong started writing a story about growing up in Thailand. This became her first novel, *Sing to the Dawn*, which she later helped to adapt into a full-length musical performed at the National Theater in Singapore. Ms. Ho's next two young adult novels were *Rice Without Rain*, based on her experience teaching in northern Thailand from 1975 to 1977, and *The Clay Marble*, the result of working with Cambodian refugees on the Thai–Cambodian border from 1980 to 1981.

Both garnered numerous awards, among them the *Booklist* Editor's Choice, Best Book for Young Adults from the American Library Association, and the Parents' Choice Award. She has also received the Southeast Asian WRITE Award from the Crown Prince of Thailand, and the Cultural Medallion from the National Arts Council in Singapore. She has also written several picture books, including *Hush! A Thai Lullaby*, which won a Caldecott Honor Award, and *Maples In the Mist*, a translation of selected Chinese Tang Dynasty poems.

Ms. Ho's short stories have been included in several anthologies, such as *Join In: Multiethnic Short Stories by Outstanding Writers for Young Adults* and *Soul-Searching Stories*. Her two forthcoming books are *Gathering the Dew*, about a young Cambodian dancer, and *Jeh-Ay! Peek-A-Boo*, a lighthearted sequel to *Hush!*

After having lived in five different countries, Ms. Ho now makes her home in Ithaca, New York, with her husband and three children. Instead of water buffaloes, there are wild turkeys and white-tailed deer in the fields outside her window. You can visit her online at www.minfongho.com.

JI-LI JIANG was born on Chinese New Year 1954, in Shanghai, China. She first became an art instructor, then a science teacher. And she had a passion for both subjects.

When Ms. Jiang came to America, she tried something totally different: She became a corporate business professional. However, she found it wasn't as much fun as she thought it would be, so she left. Now she writes books for children and talks to students at schools. Her new career perfectly combines two of her passions—art and education.

Her first book, *Red Scarf Girl*, was based on her own experiences during the Cultural Revolution, when she was twelve years old. Her powerful memoir received many awards, including ALA Best Book for

Young Adults, ALA Notable Children's Book, *Publishers Weekly* Best Book, Parents' Choice Gold Award, and ALA *Booklist* Books for Youth Editors' Choice. Her most recent book is *Magical Monkey King—Mischief in Heaven*, a retold story of the most well-known Chinese folklore.

Ms. Jiang says, "I'm not rich and famous. But I own a big heart that has an immense capacity to feel compassion and love, two essential qualities for a writer. I really love what I'm doing now, and I consider myself lucky." You can visit her online at www.jilijiang.com.

As a child, **GAIL CARSON LEVINE** lived with her older sister and her parents in the Washington Heights section of Manhattan, near her grandparents and her aunts. She wrote stories and poems through high school but had no interest in a writing career. As an adult in the 1970s, she wrote a play for children, and her husband, David, wrote the music and lyrics. The play, *Spacenapped*, was produced, way, way Off-Broadway, by a community theater in Brooklyn. Then Gail stopped writing until 1987, when she began to write stories for children. Today Gail lives with her husband and their Airedale, Baxter, in a 200-year-old farmhouse in New York's Hudson Valley. She has published eleven books for children: four novels (including *Ella Enchanted*, which won a Newbery Honor Medal in 1998), the six-book *Princess Tales* series, and the picture book *Betsy Who Cried Wolf.* You can visit her online at www.gailcarsonlevinebooks.com.

In 1965, as a young student, **BEVERLEY NAIDOO** went into exile from South Africa, where she had been imprisoned for her involvement in resistance to apartheid. She moved to England, where she married another South African exile. Dr. Naidoo has a Ph.D. related to literature and young people and an honorary doctorate. In 1985 she wrote her first children's book, *Journey to Jo'burg: A South African Story*. Although originally banned in South Africa, this acclaimed and enormously successful novel helped thousands of young readers all over the world to understand what life under apartheid meant for children. A sequel, *Chain of Fire*, followed. Dr. Naidoo is also the author of *No Turning Back*, *Out Of Bounds*, and *The Other Side of Truth*, winner of various awards, including the Carnegie Medal in 2000 and the Jane Addams Book Award in 2002. You can visit her online at www.beverleynaidoo.com.

CYNTHIA LEITICH SMITH was born on New Year's Eve 1967, during one of the worst snowstorms in Kansas City history. She spent her childhood writing poems about mice, waving gold-and-black pom-poms, talking to turtles, fishing on her great-grandpa's pontoon boat, baby-sitting a future Miss Teen U.S.A., riding horses through the Rocky Mountains, and practicing her Batgirl kicks. Cynthia had no brothers or sisters but many, many cousins (mostly girls), and an often irate Pomeranian named Sir Galahad XIII yet called Tramp. She spent her teen years popping popcorn for a movie theater, waving more pom-poms, and cruising Metcalf Avenue in her red 1968 Mustang coupe. She had better luck with grades than with boys, participated in far too many extra-curricular activities, and had unfortunate bangs.

Cynthia then earned a wonderfully economical bachelor's degree in journalism at the University of Kansas, studied abroad in Paris, and completed an overpriced law degree at the University of Michigan Law School. While a student, she worked as a waitress, cashier, newspaper reporter, public relations coordinator, and legal intern.

After graduation, Cynthia married the Keanu-esque love of her life, Greg, and later quit her law job to become a full-time writer for kids and teens. Cynthia and her husband lived for a while in an industrial-style loft in Chicago and now reside in a historic home in Austin, Texas, with their two overfed gray tabbies, Mercury and Sebastian.

Today, Cynthia is the author of *Jingle Dancer*, illustrated by Cornelius Van Wright and Ying-Hwa Hu, *Rain Is Not My Indian Name*, and *Indian Shoes*. She also has written short stories for other extremely cool anthologies. You can visit her online at www.cynthialeitichsmith.com.

DIANE STANLEY was born in Abilene, Texas, not far from her grandmother's childhood home. Her father, Burt Stanley, was a navy pilot, one of the World War II flying aces and a recipient of the Distinguished Flying Cross. Her mother, Fay Grissom, was a mystery writer. Shortly after Diane was born, her parents divorced and Fay and Diane moved to New York, then later to California. Diane graduated from Trinity University with a major in history and political science, but upon taking a life-drawing class decided to pursue a career in art. She went back to school and got a degree in medical and biological illustration from Johns Hopkins. But she wasn't a medical illustrator for long. Through her children she fell in love with children's books, and began a new career.

In 1977 her first book, *The Farmer in the Dell*, was published. Since that time she has published more than forty books, most notably her series of picture book biographies, including *Bard of Avon, Cleopatra, Leonardo da Vinci, Michelangelo,* and *Saladin: Noble Prince of Islam*. She has also explored her more playful side with picture books such as *Rumpelstiltskin's Daughter* and *Saving Sweetness*, and has written two novels for young readers, *A Time Apart* and *The Mysterious Matter of I. M. Fine*. Diane is married to Peter Vennema, who often helps with the research on her books. She has three wonderful children, Catherine, Tamara, and John. You can visit her online at www.dianestanley.com.